National Theatre C...
2021

TWO PLAYS FOR YOUN...

Find a Partner!
Like There's No Tomorrow

With introductions by
KIRSTEN ADAM and OLA ANIMASHAWUN

methuen | drama

LONDON • NEW YORK • OXFORD • NEW DELHI • SYDNEY

METHUEN DRAMA
Bloomsbury Publishing Plc
50 Bedford Square, London, WC1B 3DP, UK
1385 Broadway, New York, NY 10018, USA
29 Earlsfort Terrace, Dublin 2, Ireland

BLOOMSBURY, METHUEN DRAMA and the Methuen Drama logo are
trademarks of Bloomsbury Publishing Plc

First published in Great Britain 2021
Reprinted 2021

A catalogue record for this book is available from the British Library.

A catalog record for this book is available from the Library of Congress.

ISBN: PB: 978-1-3502-3349-2
       ePDF: 978-1-3502-3350-8
       eBook: 978-1-3502-3351-5

Series: Modern Plays

Typeset by RefineCatch Limited, Bungay, Suffolk
Printed and bound in Great Britain

To find out more about our authors and books visit www.bloomsbury.com
and sign up for our newsletters.

Contents

National Theatre Connections

Connections is the National Theatre's annual, nationwide youth theatre festival, and is a celebration of youth theatre, new writing, creativity and partnership, and above all the importance of access for young people to the arts. Every year Connections offers a unique opportunity for youth theatres and school theatre groups to stage new plays written specifically for young people, by some of the most exciting playwrights writing today, and then to perform them in leading theatres across the UK.

Our 2020 Connections cycle was cut short due to lockdown, with no Partner Theatre festivals able to take place, so we decided to carry the eight fantastic new plays we had commissioned for 2020 forward into the following year. These urgent and exciting plays – *Wind/Rush Generation(s)* by Mojisola Adebayo, *Tuesday* by Alison Carr, *A series of public apologies (in response to an unfortunate incident in the school lavatories)* by John Donnelly, *The IT* by Vivienne Franzmann, *The Marxist in Heaven* by Hattie Naylor, *Look Up* by Andrew Muir, *Crusaders* by Frances Poet, *Witches Can't Be Burned* by Silva Semerciyan – can be found in the Connections 2020 anthology.

They are joined by *Find a Partner!* by Miriam Battye and *Like There's No Tomorrow*, created by the Belgrade Young Company, Coventry, with Justine Themen, Claire Procter and Liz Mytton. We are delighted to be working with the Belgrade and showcasing the voices of their Young Company in 2021, Coventry's UK City of Culture year.

At the beginning of the rehearsal process, the National Theatre hosts the Connections Directors' Weekend – an opportunity for the directors of all the companies in the Connections programme to work with the playwright of their chosen play and a leading theatre director. Notes from these workshops accompany the plays in this anthology, giving an insight into the playwrights' intentions, creative inspiration and practical suggestions for text exploration. This year the Directors' Weekend was digitally delivered for the first time, and it was wonderful to be able to bring teachers and youth theatre leaders from around the country together online, in a time when we weren't able to meet in person.

In 2021, 200 companies from across the UK will take up the challenge of staging a Connections play, with nearly 4,000 young people, aged 13–19, involved in every aspect of theatre making. It's amazing that in these incredibly tough times for schools and theatres, Connections can still offer a space to create, to explore contemporary issues and to connect with other young theatre makers.

Connections is not just the National Theatre's programme: it is run in collaboration with theatres across the UK who are equally passionate about youth theatre. Our brilliant Partner Theatres will work with every company to develop and transfer their production, and we hope the festivals will celebrate the brilliant work that has been created and the power of theatre in these challenging times. We hope Connections 2021 will support schools and youth theatres to return to theatre making and help ensure the voices of young people are heard as theatres begin to reopen.

We hope you enjoy this year's plays and we look forward to next year and many years to come.

Kirsten Adam
Connections Producer
November 2020

Introduction

In 2016, just after the UK's referendum on membership of the European Union, I was invited to run an intensive study class with a group of writers enrolled on an MA. Many will remember that this heralded a period of highly charged national debate and introspection about, amongst other things, identity, belonging and the future. At the time, the next general election was scheduled for 2020 – so, under the title 'Your 2020 Vision' I posed this group of students the creative challenge to speculate and articulate their theatrical vision for the world in four years' time. Fascinating though their responses were to my prompting, I don't think any of them would challenge my assertion that none of them came anywhere near to what we now know actually happened in this most fateful year.

Perhaps the opposite to vision is hindsight, a skill often maligned but one which is overlooked at your peril. When you read these plays, with their scenes about entire communities not being able to breathe, and young people trapped in a circle (bubble?) and separated off, and people facing global disaster and young people crying out for a vastly different normal, etc., it would be easy to say they were created with the benefit of hindsight – but they weren't. These plays were conceived, written and completed before March 2020.

It's not that the creators of these plays had extraordinary powers of prophecy, but simply the skill of the artist, to truly look, see, listen and hear – and then tell the story of all that they surveyed. This is a phenomenon that continues to leave me breathless with awe. Namely the uncanny ability of the Connections writers and creators to read the signs, take the temperature and record the time – precisely to the second. If you really want to know the future don't consult a crystal ball, but take a good long look at these plays – because all our futures are dictated by our present. Furthermore, should you want to influence the future then extend yourself and really engage with these plays. They may not provide any answers, but they will certainly pose some piercingly provocative questions. At which point, your hindsight might just be transformed into insight.

In our lifetimes, never has a new year been so eagerly awaited, never has the need to sit down and commune been so great. The future may not be clear, but it is clear that none will need more resolve than our young. These plays invite you to sit, breathe, play and create. The future is there to be written.

Ola Animashawun
Connections Dramaturg
November 2020

The Plays

Find a Partner! *by Miriam Battye*

Hayley needs to find a boyfriend quick! She only has seconds to decide before it's too late. However, this is not real life, it's more important than that; this is a game – with strict rules. *Find a Partner!* is a play that takes us on a journey through the closing rounds of a game show about coupledom. Meet the contestants, revere them, live through them, reject them. A show played by a few and watched by many, but everyone's involved.

Who's in, who's out, who likes who, who's with who, who gets a say and who gets to choose? Everything's at stake, because, well, EVERYTHING IS AT STAKE. That's life – everybody wants a partner, don't they? No partner? Impossible to imagine ... isn't it? Impossible to live like that. Isn't it?

Like There's No Tomorrow, *created by the Belgrade Young Company with Justine Themen, Claire Procter and Liz Mytton*

There are strange cracks appearing in the land on the other side of the world, turning habitats into wastelands and creating a new wave of climate refugees. However, no one's worrying about that here – where a mayoral candidate is promising more, more, more. New industries, new jobs, new homes and masses of new stuff – all of it achieved by expansive and rapid economic growth. It's what the people want. Apart from Maru that is, whose asthma is really bad because the air is already thick with pollution, and their mantra of reduce, reuse, recycle is falling on deaf ears. Their only sanctuary is the local park. Lush and green, it's where Maru can reconnect, recharge and breathe.

However, as plans emerge to build on the park, and Maru's parents appear to be seduced by the mayoral candidate's invitation to consume as much as you can, something has to give. So, when a crack appears in Maru's new state-of-the-art bedroom furniture and then it spreads to the centre of town, and Maru seems to be the culprit, it's enough to focus everyone's attention – as they seek to deal with the symptom, whilst remaining oblivious of the cause.

Like There's No Tomorrow was created with the Belgrade Young Company, through a process of discussion, research, improvisation, scripting and revision. They first performed this play on 9 March 2020.

Find a Partner!

by Miriam Battye

Hayley needs to find a boyfriend quick! She only has seconds to decide before it's too late. However, this is not real life, it's more important than that; this is a game – with strict rules. *Find a Partner!* is a play that takes us on a journey through the closing rounds of a game show about coupledom. Meet the contestants, revere them, live through them, reject them. A show played by a few and watched by many, but everyone's involved.

Who's in, who's out, who likes who, who's with who, who gets a say and who gets to choose? Everything's at stake, because, well, EVERY THING IS AT STAKE. That's life – everybody wants a partner, don't they? No partner? Impossible to imagine . . . isn't it? Impossible to live like that. Isn't it?

Cast size

13 to 30, minimum 6M/7F
Most suitable for ages 14+

Miriam Battye is a writer from Manchester. Her play *Scenes with girls* premiered at the Royal Court in January 2020, directed by Lucy Morrison. Her other plays include *Trip the Light Fantastic* (Bristol Old Vic), *Pancake Day* (Bunker Theatre/PLAY Theatre Company) and *All Your Gold* (Theatre Royal Plymouth). She is the recipient of the 2020 Harold Pinter Commission at the Royal Court. She also writes for television. She was the first Sister Pictures Writer-in-Residence and has a number of original shows in development.

'In a cruel land, you either learn to laugh at cruelty or spend your life weeping.'

Robert Jordan

'I just want a boy who doesn't put his willy up as many girls as he wants.'

Hayley, Love Island

Characters

The Lovers

Girls:
Hayley
Jess
Sam F
Ella
Ally

Boys:
Andy
Max
Jacob
Kai
Sam M
Other Boys *(as many as you want, can double as Spectators)*

Spectators

Spectator One *(in charge)*
Other Spectators *(as many as you want)*

Notes on the Text

The game-show format that is presented in the play is metaphorical. It is reality, turned up to 100. We are watching people try to find someone to fall in love with and successfully hold onto that love through the obstacles life throws at them, whilst the whole time their love is scrutinised by people around them.

The circle in which the action happens should be simple, and needs to be no more elaborate than the outline of a large circle on the floor. The Lovers exist only within it. The Spectators exist outside it, and are the only ones who can cross the line of the circle. When they are outside the circle, no one inside can hear them. Spectator One has specified lines, and the rest can be divided amongst however many Spectators you want. Spectator One can also say lines set for other Spectators.

When the Lovers speak 'to us', they should speak directly outwards, in the direction of the real audience. These are their private thoughts, like monologues, their Diary Room of sorts. These break into the action of the play throughout, and could be realised either just with a clear turn of the head or with lighting. These can be further enhanced by having everyone else in the company watching them, for example.

The way a Lover is sent Out is up for interpretation. In this version, they are 'shot' by an unseen shotgun, and fall to the floor. You could also achieve this in different ways, physically. What matters is that they are gone from the game, for ever.

I would encourage you not to worry about the context this new reality lives in. It just is. As the play is playful and heightened I would encourage you to have fun and be playful.

Prologue: Choose Your Partner!

Three young men stand in a line, bathed in a striking light.

They are silent, quivering a little, afraid.

A young woman stands alone, a few strides away, deciding if she should choose them.

After a moment, she speaks.

Hayley   Number Two?

Boy Two *steps forward, taking a gasping breath of relief.*

The others stare on in terror.

Hayley   Yeah. I think Number Two could be my Partner.

She looks him up and down.

He looks a bit handy.
A bit helpful.
Quite fit.
Not so fit that I'd be in a constant state of threat.
And not so un-fit that he'd bring our average down.
He has the fitness of someone who would love me about 10 per cent more than I love him.
And that's all anyone wants, really.

He smiles, grateful.

Boy Two   I'm *so grateful* you chose me.

Hayley   Aw.

She smiles.

Her smile falls.

Oh. Actually. Can you just turn your head again?

He turns his head a little to the side, worried.

Oh. Oh no.
You see that?
He's got a slightly deviated jaw line there? It's fine now but that's an early sign that his kids are gonna be crap at sports.

She looks at the camera/audience.

Mama don't want nerds.

He shakes his head, frantically.

She looks back at him.

Plus his plimsolls make him look like a wanker.

So I'll go with Number Three.

Boy Two *shakes his head, makes a few desperate sounds, but she has spoken.*

Boy Three *gratefully steps forward as* **Boy Two** *steps back.*

Boy Three   Omigod! Thank you.

Hayley   Hiya! – Yeah. Number Three's my final choice.

She holds out her hand. He steps forward, gratefully takes it in his.

The **Spectators** *have been watching intently from outside the circle. They move freely around it.*

One of them steps into the circle from the outside, addresses the remaining boys. This is **Spectator One***, and they are very much in charge of proceedings.*

Spectator One   So, guys. No one wants to be your Partner. I'm sorry . . . you're Out! Time to say goodbye!

The remaining boys are shot, one by one, by an unseen gun.

They are Out.

They fall to the floor one by one.

Hayley *looks out at us, the audience.*

Hayley   I'm not picky. I just value myself.

Hayley *and* **Boy Three** *assemble themselves in a Partner pose, joining the other Lovers.*

(Perhaps lights up to reveal) They are assembled in sets of Partners, all standing in their Partner poses. Coupley. Happy.

Spectator One   So you've all found a Partner. Now the real game begins! Who'll be Out next? Who's gonna lose, and who's gonna –

All   WIN AT LOVE!

The Partners fist pump the air together –

All   GOOOOO LOVE!

With a musical flourish, we move straight into –

Part One: Why Love?

The monologues happen out to us, the audience.

Everyone watches the Partner duo who are speaking.

During the monologues, the bodies of the two rejected boys are dragged off out of the circle by their feet, clumsily, by **Spectators***. A* **Spectator** *wipes the floor where they were with blue roll.*

Jess *and* **Andy.**

Jess *speaks to us. She is bold, pragmatic.*

Jess   Why do I want a Partner?

She thinks.

Well. I've been Unpartnered for about . . . six months now?
And it's starting to become a problem.
People are starting to get – *uncomfortable.*
When I don't have a satisfactory answer to *the Question.*

She pauses.

It's getting hard to avoid *the Question.*

She pauses.

'Are you seeing anyone?'
'Got a Partner yet, hun?'
'Are you maybe just too picky, darling, cos my niece has got chronic impetigo and
even she's got one . . .'

She nods her head, a greater resolve.

So yeah.
That's why I'm here.
It's time to get a Partner.
It's time to get Loved.

All   GOOOOO LOVE!

Andy *speaks to us. He is furtive, wildly anxious.*

Andy   It's not like I haven't tried to find one.
I'm on every app –
I go to every social event –
I maintain open body language, at all times –
I haven't crossed my arms in three years –
I spend a lot of time standing in lifts, actually, just, waiting –
Always keep a seat next to me at weddings –
At the cinema –
On the bus –
Just in case. Someone just happens to . . . fill it
And we can start, y'know, Falling in Love.

A brief silence.

He gets a bit breathy, sensing he's not proved himself enough –

I BAKE.
I listen to FEMINIST PODCASTS.
I am consistently VERY NICE to everyone I meet –

Trust me, I've tried EVERYTHING.

A breath.

This really is my last chance.
Cos you *have* to find a Partner here, right?
Or you're Out.

He pauses. To take a breath. To contemplate death.

(*To himself.*) Ohhh, this might have been a mistake.

Jess *pipes up, speaks to us –*

Jess   I just feel like I have all this Love just ready and waiting.
Fully formed. Beautiful and massive and life-changing.
And I don't have anyone to, like, give it to.

Andy *looks at her.*

Andy   Me too. I feel that way too.

They look at each other.

Andy   Go Love?

All   GOOOOO LOVE!

*The **Spectators** call out their responses outside the circle. They cannot be heard by those inside.*

Spectator One   What do you think, guys?

Spectator   I think the standard is really going downhill TBH

Spectator   Yeah I can't wank to any of these

Spectator   It looks like they've just gone into the canteen and grabbed whoever didn't have their mouth full

Spectator   It looks like they've just rounded up some dogs and kicked them through Matalan

*The **Spectators** laugh.*

Spectator   Shut up! They still deserve a Partner. Everyone, no matter how unlovable, deserves a Partner

Spectator   Disagree. No one wants to see uglies bumping their actually ugly uglies

*The **Spectators** laugh.*

Sam F *and* **Max**.

Max *speaks to us. He is unwaveringly cocksure.*

Max   I'm not even Unpartnered now.
I'm fighting them off.

No, literally, I am *fighting* them off.
I've had to put up fences.
I've had to put up walls.
I've got a sixteen-metre perimeter around my house so that girls can't break in to my bathroom.
I regularly cause traffic jams –
I've caused three semi-serious collisions just getting myself a Pret.
I've been banned from most shopping centres.
I don't even get the bus.
I just – crowd-surf to my destination.
I'm here to win. Obv.
What else am I going to do with all of this? Politics?

He thinks.

Max (*to himself*)   Maybe I should do Politics.

Sam F *looks at* **Max** *for a moment, disturbed. He notices.*

Max   What?

Sam F *looks back to us. She speaks. She is grounded, realistic.*

Sam F   I just want to find out if I really need a Partner or not.
Cos if I'm honest I have no idea if I do, or if someone has just told me I do.
I want to know if Partnering Up still holds the societal capital it had in the past,
Or whether we're free, now, to decide who or what we need to make us happy.

Max *looks at her, disturbed.*

Sam F   What?

Spectator   I give these guys a week

Spectator   Yeah. She's boring and he's the human equivalent of splashback

Spectator   I'd let him splash my back

The **Spectators** *laugh.*

Spectator   He'll be a shit Partner though

Spectator   Yeah he'll be shit at Love, he won't know what to do with it

Spectator   I reckon she can change him y'know

Spectator   Omigod – Project!

All Spectators   GOTTALOVEADICKHEAD

Ella *and* **Jacob**.

Jacob *speaks to us. He is trying his best to be cool about this.*

Jacob   Um. I'm here because I think I need some guidance?

Like what do I say. Exactly. To keep her.
I mean I'm not worried.
I mean I'm totally fine.

He briefly pauses.

It's just my armpits that betray me.

He touches an armpit. Rubs his fingers together. Drenched with sweat.

He holds it out to us. Please.

I just need someone to tell me what to do. And then what to do after I've done that. And then what to do after I've done that. And how not to be terrified about all of it.

Spectator   This guy is desperado

Spectator   Big time

Spectator   Big Desperate Energy

Spectator   You can see it in his eyes –

Spectator   see it a mile off –

All Spectators   PANTY SNIFFER

Spectator One *jumps into the circle, addresses* **Jacob** –

Spectator One   Okay, okay, Jacob, honesty is great, everyone loves honesty, but I think, possibly, you need to say something a bit less sadboy?

Jacob   Wwwwhat do you mean?

Spectator One   Y'know, bit more 'awwwite'? Bit more 'get in there lads'? Bit more 'cuppla-pints-and-some-pawwwk-scratchings'-type of okay with yourself?

Another **Spectator** *jumps in.*

Spectator   Yeah otherwise you'll be Out sooner than you can say 'prescription strength deodorant'

Jacob *turns back and speaks to us* –

Jacob   I've come because I'm reasonably lonely?

Spectator One   Mmm no it's a bit –

Jacob   I really like girls and I want one I want one I want one in my tum?

Spectator   Well, that's just a bit weird, but –

Jacob   Just. Tell me what to say. Just tell me. And I'll say it.

Another **Spectator** *jumps in.*

Spectator   Maybe just keep your mouth shut, hun.

Jacob *does. He does double thumbs up.*

The **Spectators** *all jump out of the circle, and watch.*

Ella *speaks to us. She makes a lot of 'air quote' gestures.*

Ella   Well. I've never been very 'popular'. I've never been particularly good at 'people'. I've never really understood 'romantic comedies' or 'love songs' or what the fuck makes 'will they won't they' so interesting – like – will they, or won't they? Like, answer the question.

The main thing is even if they will at the beginning, eventually they won't.
So shut the fuck up about it.

She thinks.

It's not that I'm 'cynical'. I'm just *aware* of people's self-interest and therefore *generally* mistrustful of people's intentions?

She thinks.

Okay fine, I am cynical.
Whatever. I'm a child of divorce. And *East Enders*.

A brief pause.

Jacob *does a thumbs up at her, hopeful. She frowns.*

Spectator   Dunno if she deserves a Partner actually

Spectator   Yeah. Leave 'Love' to the 'optimists'. 'Hun'.

Spectator   I call bullshit. It's always the ones who claim they don't want Love who are doing boy raindances and poking holes in condoms

The **Spectators** *laugh.*

Ally *and* **Kai** *speak to us. They are a bit confused.*

Ally   Um. I'd just quite like a Partner?

Kai   I'd just quite like a Partner too?

They look at each other.

Ally   This might work.

Ally *looks back at us, smiling brightly.*

I have very low expectations.

Kai *grins.*

Everyone is standing in their Partner poses. Smiling.

Jess (*smiling*)   Does anyone know what we do now?

Andy (*smiling*)   I dunno. Just keep smiling.

Hayley (*smiling*)   Are we supposed to start arguing yet?

Ella (*smiling*)   I think that comes later?

Jess (*leaning out to speak to* **Sam F**, *psst*)   Oi, Sam? What type are you?

Sam F   What, sorry?

Jess   Like you were talking about 'societal capital' does that mean you're the boring type?

Sam F   What?

Jess   Like Hayley's the fit type, I'm the damaged type, Ella is . . .

Ella   I'm the bitch, I think?

Jess   Right, and Ally's the thick type.

Ally (*waving at* **Sam F**)   Helloooo!

Jess   We're all different types.

Ella   Yeah it's kinda like the Spice Girls, but not like really old.

Sam F (*to* **Jess**)   You're the . . . damaged type?

Jess   Oh yeah. You've got to be a bit damaged. You've got to have been, like, hurt before. Otherwise you won't know the red flags. Otherwise you'll fall for the first person who says you've got nice teeth.

Sam F   Who decided this, sorry?

Jess   It's just good sense to know your type.

Ella   Like, how can you be anyone's type if you don't know what type you are?

Sam   So . . . what about the boys?

Jess *points the boys out one by one* (**Max**, **Boy Number Three**, **Jacob**, **Andy**, **Kai**, *back to* **Andy**.)

Jess   Ummm . . . Tosser, tosser, tosser, not, not, probably not.

Sam   That's it?

Jess   Ummm. Boys are simple.

Sam   Are they?

Spectator   What the hell is going on? Where's the drama? Is anyone else getting – BORED

The **Spectator** *turns their back to the circle. Followed by –*

Spectator (*turning their back*)   Yep, BORED

Spectator One *jumps into the circle.*

Spectator One   Guys, what are you waiting for?

Can you just shut up and get on with it please?

They run out of the circle.

Sam F   Wait – what?

Ella   What are we getting on with?

Spectator One *jumps back in again.*

Spectator One   Falling in Love, of course!
On your marks . . . get set . . .

All   GOOOOOO LOVE!

Part Two: Fall in Love!

The contestants set about Falling in Love in the circle. The **Spectators** *watch intently.*

How would you try to 'fall in love' if you had limited time? It could be a physical movement, proximity, trying to telepathically link, running or throwing yourself at each other; it could be trying to learn everything about each other straight away. Every Partnership tries to work it out.

Ella *and* **Jacob**. *Sitting, staring at each other. Trying to fall in love.*

Ella   What do we need to do?

Jacob   Fall in love.

Ella   I think the most important thing is. Proximity.

They look at each other. They shuffle closer to each other.

Jacob   Done.

Ella   And having compatible personalities.

Jacob   How do we do that?

Ella (*serious*)   I'm really bubbly.

Jacob   I'm not. So that's a good balance?

Ella   Right, and sharing the same values.

Jacob   Okay. Are you happy with your values?

Ella   Yes.

Jacob   Cool, I'll share them.

Ella   Nice.

Jacob   We're really nailing this. Love you.

Ella   No that's too soon. It has to be believable.

Jacob (*not understanding*)   Oh right. I get you. And I looo –

Ella   No.

Jacob   Sorry.

He touches his armpit. It's sodden.

Jacob   Shit.

Jess *and* **Andy**. *Standing, looking at each other.*

Jess   This is going to be hard work.

Andy   Relationships are supposed to be hard work.

Jess   Give and take.

Andy   Commitment. Compromise. It might be painful but it's worth it.

Jess   Otherwise we'll be single.

Andy   We'll be *single people*.

Jess   You can't get a mortgage on a *single person's* salary

Andy   Who are you supposed to kiss on New Year's Eve?

Jess   Who are you supposed to talk to? Your family and friends?

Andy   Who are you supposed to talk to your family and friends *about*?

Jess   Yeah.

Andy   Yeah.

Jess   I agree.

Andy   Totally.

A pause. They look at each other.

Jess   I think we might be quite compatible, actually.

They high ten, elated.

Andy   Amazing. Can this be our thing?

Jess   Absolutely.

They high ten again.

Jess and Andy   WE HAVE A THING!

Hayley *and* **Boy Three**. *Standing. She is inspecting him. He is nervous, afraid to fuck up.*

Hayley   Do you have a history of mental illness in the family?

He shakes his head.

Diabetes?

He shakes his head.

Male pattern baldness?

He looks up at his own head. He shakes his head.

Hayley   Oh so are you like a secretly hairy family?

Boy Three   No, we have like a normal amount of hair.

Hayley   And have you got your own teeth?

He nods his head.

Hayley   Can I have a look?

Boy Three   You – want to look at my teeth?

Hayley   Yeah.

Boy Three   Umm.

Hayley   Unless . . . you've got something to hide?

He opens his mouth immediately.

She looks at them.

Hayley   What's your name by the way?

Boy Three (*mouth open*)   Joey.

Hayley   What?

He closes his mouth.

Boy Three   Joey.

She frowns.

Hayley   Well, that's not gonna work is it?

Boy Three   Why not?

Hayley   What's our Partner name gonna be? 'Hoey'?

Boy Three   Uhhhhhh . . .

Hayley *looks around, calls out –*

Hayley   When are we getting new boys in, people?

Boy Three   No no no no. I can change my name! I just won't have a name! You can just have all the – name. You don't even have to look at me. We can just pretend I don't exist.

He crouches into a little ball, covering his head –

Boy Three   See? This is totally sustainable.

Hayley   Fine. I mean there's no one else anyway.

Boy Three *looks up at her, exhales, relieved.*

Boy Three   Do we kiss now?

Hayley *thinks for a moment. Rolls her eyes, relents.*

Hayley   Fine.

He goes to stand to go for a kiss; she puts up a fist. He stops, confused, and kisses her knuckles.

He goes back down and holds himself in a little ball, sobbing quietly.

Max *and* **Sam F**. *Standing.* **Max** *is basically ignoring her.*

Sam F   So. Like. What are your interests?

Max   I don't understand what's happening right now.

Sam F   Um. We're having a conversation.

Max   I don't normally have to. Conversation.

Sam F   Can you just try? *What are you interests?*

He stares at her for a moment.

Max   I don't know.

He really struggles.

Max   I quite like old boats.

Sam F   Yeah?

Max   Nah not really actually.

Sam F   Right. Great.
Now you ask me a question.

He stares, blankly.

Max   I normally just like vaguely insult girls.
Liiiike –
'You look better than usual.'

He pauses for effect.

Do you Love me now?

She stands up.

Sam F   Okay I can't do this.

Max   Wow, you're really different from other girls.

Sam   Am I?

Max   You really, like, challenge me!

She suddenly runs, full pelt out of the circle – but bumps into the imaginary wall of the chalk circle.

She falls back, in pain.

Sam F   Ow!

Spectator   Lol where does she think she's going

Sam F (*to herself*)   Argh. What am I gonna do?

A **Spectator** *jumps into the circle to give advice.*

Spectator   You've got to give him a chance, hun.

Sam F   But. I hate him.

Another jumps in.

Spectator   I think you're being a bit harsh TBH. Like, he's probably just got his guard up.

Spectator   Yeah he probably just has a bad relationship with his mum or whatever and struggles to trust women.

Spectator   Yeah! Exactly! Just try to connect with him.

Sam F   I cannot connect with that. There is nothing to connect – to.

Spectator   Well, you could be less of a bitch? I think you'd work better as like a . . . Wise, sage type? Sort of like . . . an old goose or something. Or your nan. Ok?

Sam F   What?

Spectator   Just BE NICE.
(*Whispering.*) Otherwise you're Out, babes.

The **Spectators** *jump out of the circle.* **Sam F** *returns to sit beside* **Max***. She tries to be nice.*

Ally *and* **Kai***. Standing. Facing each other. They are calm. Zen.*

Spectator   What are they . . . doing?

The **Spectators** *peer at* **Ally** *and* **Kai** *from outside the circle.*

Spectator   Is she already giving him the silent treatment?

Spectator   Is this passive aggressive or aggressive aggressive?

Spectator   No . . . she's pissed *him* off

Spectator   I think they're *both* angry

Suddenly –

Kai   Go!

They start play fighting and wrestling.

Spectator   Ooh! Violence!

A bored **Spectator** *tuns back around to the circle to watch.*

Spectator   OOH!

Ally *pins* **Kai** *down. They erupt into giggles.*

Ally   I win!

Kai   Argh, dammit!

They sit together, giggling.

A **Spectator** *jumps into the circle.*

Spectator   Um. What's going on here? Who's mad at who?

Kai   What?

Ally   We're not mad

Spectator   So what you're just. Having a nice time.

Ally   Yeah.

Spectator   You're just. Getting on.

Kai   Yeah.

Ally *nods, smiling.*

Ally   Yeah!

Her face falls.

Sorry. Is that not okay?

The **Spectator** *jumps out of the circle again.*

Spectator   We need them Out, asap

Spectator   I think it's cute

Spectator   I think it's *too* cute

Spectator   Yeah. They're definitely faking it

All Spectators   GAME PLAN

They watch all the Partners assembled in the circle, who are messing around, chatting, ignoring each other.

Spectator   I think everyone likes each other a bit too much actually

Spectator   Yeah I'm sorry but I can't invest in a relationship if it hasn't been tested a bit

Spectator   BORED

The bored **Spectator** *turns their back on the circle. Another follows suit.*

Spectator (*turning their back*)   BORED

Spectator One   I know –

Spectator One *suddenly shoves* **Sam M** (*male*) *from outside the circle into the circle and everyone gasps.*

Sam M   Hey, guys, I'm Sam!

All Spectators   Oooooooooooh

Spectator   TWIST.

Sam M *is going round introducing himself. 'Hi, I'm Sam. Hi, I'm Sam. Hi, I'm Sam', etc.*

Hayley   Hi, I'm Hayley.

Sam M   Hi, I'm Sam.

Hayley *turns and speaks to us.*

Hayley   Yeah so I'm getting like a medium vibe with Sam.

Sam M *shakes* **Ella** *and* **Jacob***'s hands.*

Sam M   Hi I'm Sam, hi I'm Sam.

Jacob *turns to speak to us, still shaking* **Sam M***'s hand.*

Jacob   I'm not threatened by new boy Sam, no.
Me and Ella are really happy.
Really calm and happy.
Yeah.
Yeah.

A pause. He nods a lot.

I haven't pooed in three days though, so.

They stop shaking hands.

Sam M *wipes his hand on his trousers.*

Sam F *holds out her hand to* **Sam M**.

Sam F   Hi, I'm Sam!

Sam M   Hi, I'm also Sam!

Hayley   Omigod that's hilarious. What would your Partner name be? 'Sam'?

She laughs a lot.

Sam F (*sarcastic*)   I guess we can't be Partners then, Hayley.

Hayley   Wow, that was like, reallyveryrude.

Max *shakes* **Sam**'s *hand.*

Sam M   Hi, I'm Sam.

Max *talks to us –*

Max   Absolutely no threat there. He's not going to steal Girl Sam from me.

I mean I'm not even bothered if he does. I'm keeping my options open, if you know what I mean. Not putting *all my eggs in one breakfast*, if you know what I mean. I mean I'll cross that bridge *when I cross it*, if you know what I mean. I mean if you know *what I mean*, if you know what I mean.

A **Spectator** *steps into the circle.*

Spectator   What do you mean?

Max *thinks.*

Max   I dunno.

He doesn't know what to do, so goes with –

Max (*laddy*)   Tits! I dunno.

He sits on the floor, a bit tired.

Sam M *goes to* **Sam F**, *who is standing alone at the edge of the circle, looking for a way out.*

Sam M   Hi, other Sam. You ok?

Sam F   You don't have to talk to me. I'm not your Partner.

Sam M   No I know I just. Felt like saying hello. You seem kind of normal.

Sam F   D'you reckon we could be friends?

He looks at her. He looks around.

Sam M   Is that allowed?

Spectator (*peering at them from outside the circle*)   Don't like that

Spectator   Yeah what *is* that?

Spectator   Sam is such a dark horse!

Spectator   How *dare* he try and steal a Partner!

Spectator   Well, he doesn't want to be Out. Who do we want Out?

Spectator One *jumps into the circle. Speaks brightly –*

Spectator One   Right, grab your Partner, let's see who's still in Love!

The Lovers all grab their Partners, get into their poses, whilst asking –

Jess   Wait, I thought it was to find out who's the Most Loved?

Ella   No I think it's who's the Best at Love?

Jacob   I thought it was whose Love *is* the Best?

Andy   Is there a difference?

Jess   The main thing is we're not Out.
(*To* **Andy**.) I'm not gonna be Out, am I?

Andy (*dead serious*)   Of course not. I'm falling in love with you.

Jess (*serious*)   I'm falling in love with you too.

Andy   Good. On schedule.

They high ten, serious. Clasp each other tight.

Sam M *looks around, terrified.*

Sam M   Wait wait wait. I don't have a Partner.

He appeals to the girls, a little frantic –

Sam M   I think I'd be a really good Partner. I'm really dependable, and I'm a good listener, and I like . . . travelling and, dogs-and-or-cats and, documentaries and . . . it doesn't matter, the main thing is I won't leave you. I'll just – stay – with you. And you'll never be Out.

Hayley *suddenly steps forward.*

Hayley   I'll take him!

Sam M *spins round to her.*

Sam M   What?

Boy Three   *What!*

He immediately falls to his knees in horror and sadness and the rage of futile mortality.

Spectator One   Um. Can we at least give it a *bit* of a tense pause?

Hayley *goes back to her Partner and pulls up a gasping, panicking* **Boy Three**, *linking arms with him.* **Spectator One** *looks at* **Boy Three.**

Spectator One   Okay *you* need to look less worried, because you don't know what she's going to do yet.

Boy Three   But.
But you're about to – I'm about to –

He looks around, for help.

No one says anything.

He relents. Starting to cry, he puts on a smile.

Spectator One   Thank you. So!
Would anyone like to swap Partners?

Hayley *pretends to grapple with the decision.*

Hayley   Ummmm I –

She steps forward and **Boy Three** *holds onto her arm, tugging her back. A little tustle.*

She wrenches free –

Hayley   I do!

Everyone, **Spectators** *and all, pretend to gasp.*

Hayley   I'm sorry, but I might be *happier* with Sam. What do you want me to do? Possibly *not* be happier?

She joins **Sam M**. **Boy Three** *is left alone, crying quietly. He crawls around, trying to find the exit.*

Spectator   Can you blame her? That boy is human cartilage and we all know it

Spectator   She was the only one bringing the sauce in that relationship

Spectator   He definitely loved her more than she loved him. Say it with me –

All Spectators   PRECARIOUS

Hayley   What happens now? Did I win yet?

Andy   Yeah who won this round?

Spectator One   What do we reckon, guys? Who's the Best so far?

All the **Spectators** *shrug. 'Whatever, don't care, you pick', etc.*

Spectator One *jumps back into the circle.*

Spectator One   The Best Partners are . . . HAYLEY AND SAM!

All Spectators   GOOOOO HAM!

Hayley *screams and jumps up and down, hugging* **Sam M**, *who is baffled.*

Sam M   But we literally just met?

Hayley   *Shut up.*

Spectator One   How do you feel?

Hayley   Uh, the Best?

A bit of jumping up and down from **Hayley**, *alone.*

Jess   Okay so who's Out?

Spectator One *jumps outs and addresses the other* **Spectators**.

Spectator One   What do you reckon, chaps?

They all decisively point at **Ally** *and* **Kai**.

Spectator One *jumps back in.*

Spectator One   It's Ally and Kai!

A confused pause. Some of the **Spectators** *makes 'aw' sounds.*

Jess *and* **Andy** *secretly high ten.*

Spectator One *does a big sad face at* **Ally** *and* **Kai**.

Spectator One   Aw, guys. Sad times.

Kai   Wait, what's happening?

Ally   We're the Most Loved Partners?

Spectator One   No. The Least. *Least Loved.* Where do you think it all went wrong?

Ally   Um. What? Oh, I don't know. I don't know. I really liked him.

Kai   Yeah, me too.

Spectator One *can't resist an 'aw'.*

Spectator One   Omigod. Gutted.

Spectator One *yells up to some unseen overlords.*

Spectator One   Can we have some gutted music please?

Gutted music plays.

Spectator One   So Ally. You can be Out with Kai. Or you can save yourself. If you want to Partner with . . . whatever his name is.

Boy Three (*quietly, forlornly*)   Joey.

Spectator One   What are you going to do?

Ally *looks at* **Kai**.

Ally   Well. I choose Kai. Of course I choose Kai. I really like him. I like, *like* like him.

Kai   You do?

Ally   Yeah. I mean. I don't know what like liking is or anything but. Yeah. They say you know when you know don't you? So maybe I know.

A brief pause.

Ally (*shrugging*)   I dunno.

They hold each other's hands.

Kai   Me too. Me neither.

They smile at each other.

Spectator One   Aw.

Spectator   Bless

Spectator   That's actually quite cute

They hold hands, looking at each other, happy, loving.

Spectator One   Wow. That is commitment, isn't it?
I mean it's *so* nice in a way because you actually *know* now, for sure that it's real.

Ally and Kai   Yeah.

Spectator One   This relationship *is* real.

Ally and Kai   Yeah.

Spectator One   Since you're Out anyway.

Ally and Kai   Yeah.

A brief pause.

Ally   Wait, what?

They are shot. They are Out. One by one, they hit the floor.

A pause.

Boy Three   Um –

He is shot. He is Out. He hits the floor.

A brief pause.

Spectator   Great!

Lights change. Their bodies are cleared away with brisk efficiency. Someone wipes down the floor where they were with blue roll.

During this, **Sam F** *moves to the edge and knocks on the circle.*

Spectator One *jumps into the circle to talk to her.*

Sam F   If they *actually* loved each other, doesn't that defeat the point of this whole thing? Shouldn't they have won?

Spectator One   Well, no, because. They were the worst at Love.

Sam F   But why?

Spectator One *thinks.*

Spectator One   It was just too *easy* for Ally and Kai. There wasn't enough of a journey. To win at Love, you've got to be the best Partners.

Sam F   The best Partners.

Spectator One   Yes, the best Partners.

Sam F   How do we do that? Are you just changing the rules as we go?

Spectator One   Rules? There aren't any *rules*, hun. Love doesn't play by the rules.

Which leads us straight into –

Part Three: Be in Love!

Spectator One *addresses the Lovers.*

Spectator One   You've found a Partner. And you've fallen in Love, it's time for the biggest challenge of all. Being in Love.

General confusion from the Lovers.

Spectator One   What will your Love look like? How will you keep it? How will you manage it, and take care of it? Time to find out. On your marks . . . get set . . .

All   GOOOOOO LOVE!

Andy *and* **Jess**. *Walking around an imaginary home.*

Andy   So this is where we'll put the fridge. And the new cupboards. And the oven –

Jess   We'll argue about whether we get a gas or fan-assisted –

Andy   This is where I'll make you try my Bolognese –

He does. She does. It is too hot. They laugh.

Jess   My mum will email you over that recipe you wanted –

Andy   Ah, love your mum –

Jess (*to herself*)   Mum will be so happy I've finally found someone . . .

Andy   We'll put the dining table here –

Jess   Yes!

They sit at it. They quickly talk through their lives –

Andy   This is where we'll argue –

Jess   About money –

Andy   About priorities –

Jess   About that woman at work –

Andy   About what to do about your dad now he's –

Jess   This is where you'll tell me I look beautiful even if I don't –

Andy   Where you'll tell me I look beautiful because you know I need to hear it –

Jess   This is where you'll hurt me. You'll hurt me here too. And here.

Andy   And me here, here. This is where you won't even mean to.

Jess   This is where I'll feel like I'm finally in my own home instead of just a visitor in it –

Andy   This is where I'll get the proof I needed –

Jess   This is where you'll never leave me even if you want to –

Andy   This is where I won't want to –

This is where the commitment will live –

Jess   Yes this is where the happiness will sit –

Andy   Yes this is where we'll look at it and polish it and own it –

Jess   This is where we'll take care of it –

Andy   Good. Thank you.

Jess   I feel better now. I can relax now.

They hold each other in their home. They try to relax.

Jacob *and* **Ella**. *Slow dancing. He talks covertly to the* **Spectators** *over her shoulder as they go round.*

Jacob   Hello? What do I do now? How do I keep my Partner?

Spectators *pop into the circle to offer advice –*

Spectator   Have you said I Love You yet?

Jacob   Yes!

Spectator   Great! Then you can relax.

Jacob   Well, *I've* said it. She's a bit resistant.

Spectator   Oh no. Then stop relaxing. Stop relaxing right now. You can't say that and not hear it back.

Spectator   Yeah that's really sad, mate

Spectator   You've just gotta get those words out of her. If you get her to say it, she might start to mean it.

Jacob   Okay. Okay. I will.

*The **Spectators** jump out of the circle.*

Spectator   Is that how it works?

Spectator (*shrugging*)   Dunno. Guess we're about to find out.

They watch.

Jacob   Can't you just tell me you love me?

Ella   Why?

Jacob   Because I told you I love you.

Ella   Is that the reason people tell each other that?

Jacob   I just need to hear it.

Ella   Okay. Say I did love you. But telling you I love you all the time isn't part of the way I love. I struggle saying it. Would that be okay?

Jacob *thinks.*

Jacob   Can't you just say it?

Ella *thinks. She relents. She sees how much he needs it.*

Ella   Okay. I love you.

Jacob   Thank you.
Wasn't that easy?

Sam M *and* **Hayley**. **Hayley** *is quite enthusiastic.* **Sam M** *isn't.*

Hayley   What do you think our Being in Love will look like? Should we like. Pretend get a dog? Pretend go on holiday? We could pretend do anything!

Sam M   Why don't we just pretend slow down a bit and pretend have a conversation first.

Hayley   Okay. What should we talk about?

Sam M   Can't we just. Pretend? Like. Pretend talk. Pretend joke. Pretend laugh. There you go. Look how much we're pretend nailing it.

Hayley   Don't you want to, actually get to know me?

Sam M   Look. No offence, Hayley, I'm sure you're very nice.
But I just want to get through this without getting Out.
Feel like if we start getting to know each other, we're gonna find out we don't like each other, we'll start fighting, and then we'll *want* each other Out.

Hayley (*disappointed*)   D'you really think so?

Sam M   I said I would stay your Partner. So I will.
Just. Don't make it hard for me.

Hayley *pauses. She is hurt.*

Hayley   Okay. Sorry.

They pretend hold hands. Sad.

*The **Spectators** are watching intently.*

Spectator   Okay, is anyone starting to quite like them?

Spectator   They do say honesty is the root of the best relationships

Spectator   Yeah I could totally watch them hate–love each other all day

Spectator   I want more Max action. I love him. IWishICouldSpreadHimOnABagel

Spectator   Bin Girl Sam though

Spectator   Yeah Girl Sam is such a failed example of carbon she actually makes me want to never have kids

Spectator (*turning around*)   Oh here she is, I'm already BORED

Spectator (*turning around*)   BORED

Sam F *and* **Max**. *Sitting. Silent.*

Max   Right, shall we have a go at a conversation again? I've thought of a question.

Sam F   It's taken you this long to think of a question?

Max   Sorry. This is all new for me!

Sam F   I feel like everyone else is a lot further along than we are. Ella and Jacob have said the L word, Jess and Andy have got a whole *life* laid out and we're still trying to string a conversation together?

She stands up and walks away.

Max   I'm sorry, I just – you're quite intimidating!

He hangs his head in shame. Maybe starts exercising.

Sam M *breaks away from* **Hayley** *and meets* **Sam F** *in the centre of the circle.*

Sam M   You all right?

Sam F   Yeah, great, thanks, You?

They both resort to heavy sarcasm.

Sam M   Great. Totally great.

Sam F   Yeah I'm really enjoying myself.

Sam M   Yeah I'm literally so in love it's crazy.

Sam F   Yeah I can't eat, sleep, think about anything other than him,

Sam M   I'm actually struggling to form sentences.

Sam F   Me too! I feel like I'm *high*.

Sam M   Oh yeahhh my stomach and lungs and all vital organs are full of butterflies!

Sam F   Omigod, me too, and candy floss, and fairy dust, and fucking. Taylor Swift songs.

Sam M   I feel like I could just burst into song at any moment!

They are both laughing now. They come to a stop.

Sam M   Wow. I haven't laughed in so long I'd actually forgotten what that was.

Sam F   Oh crap. Are people going to think something is 'happening' between us now.

Sam M   Inevitably.

Sam F   When did that happen? When did everything start meaning so much?

Sam M   I dunno.

Sam F   I thought Love was supposed to be fun. And maybe vaguely relaxing. I just feel more stressed than before.

Sam M   Ditto.

A brief pause.

Sam M and Sam F   Deeeep.

They laugh a little.

Sam F   I think we are definitely friends now.

He looks at her.

Sam M   I'd fucking love to be your friend, Girl Sam.

Sam F   Thanks, Boy Sam.

They hug, friends, laughing a little.

Spectator One *talks to another* **Spectator** *outside the circle.*

Spectator   What is going on there?

Spectator One   Are they Partners?

Spectator   I think they're friends.

Spectator One   That doesn't count. So they're potential Partners.

Spectator   What do you mean?

Spectator One   They're a boy and a girl, right? They're –

Spectator   Yeah.

The other **Spectator** *looks at them dumbly.*

Spectator One   Well, then.

Spectator One *places their hands on an imaginary surface in front. They push it forward.*

Spectator One   Give them a little. Push.

By this point, all the Partners have started trying to ballroom dance together, with varying levels of success.

A **Spectator** *goes up behind* **Max**, *who is dancing generically on his own, and nudges him.*

Spectator   Hey what's going on with Sam and Sam?

Max   What?

They point at **Sam F** *and* **Sam M**, *who are dancing together, laughing.*

Spectator   There.

Max   What do you mean?

Another **Spectator** *jumps into the circle.*

Spectator   She's making you look a mug, mate.

They pat **Max** *and push him forward.*

Spectator (*whispers into his ear*)   Also Jacob said you have little tiny boy legs.

Max *is immediately revved up. He is pushed towards* **Sam F** *and* **Sam M**.

The **Spectators** *retreats out of the circle and watch.*

Max   What do you think you're doing, dickhead?

Sam M *turns to* **Max**, *surprised.*

Sam M   What what where?

Max   With her.

Sam M   Sam?

Max   Watch your back, mate.

Sam M   Why?

Max   Wolf in snake's clothing, mate. Wolf. In snake's clothing.

He thinks about this.

Sam M   I think you'd – probably still be able to tell it was a wolf if it was, like, in a snake's –

Sam F   Are we not allowed to have a conversation?

Jess   No, you're not allowed to do that.

Sam F   Why not?

Jess   I dunno, it's just really uncool of you.

Sam F   What kind of arbitrary morality is this?

Hayley   Why are you using the words 'arbitrary morality' – seriously WHO DO YOU THINK YOU'RE TALKING TO?

Jacob   Whoah whoah whoah what's going on here?

Ella   Wait, is Boy Sam partnering with Girl Sam now?

Sam F   We're just having a conversation! We're literally just friends, I have no interest in him like that!

Sam M *looks at her, a little forlorn.*

Hayley   I AM – NOT – GOING – OUT.

She points at **Sam M***, hard.*

Hayley   YOU PROMISED.

Spectator One   Time to light a match under it –

They run into the circle.

Spectator One   ALL RIGHT ALL RIGHT ALL RIGHT
It's time to swap Partners!

Sam F   What? Now?

Jacob   Why?

Max   Yeah, why?

Jess   Why are you doing this now? I like my Partner! I don't want to have to do it all again. I'm exhausted, I'm *exhausted*, Partnering up is *exhausting*. I just want to stay with this one!

Spectator One   But you want to be *sure* don't you?

Jess   Sure about what?

Spectator One   That you really Love each other, of course? That you're a real, valid, real-life, proper, never going to break up, real life, shitting-with-the-door-open, fucking, couple.

A brief pause.

Spectator One   This is all in your interests, isn't it? You know this is all for you, right?

Jess *thinks. She is a bit baffled.*

Jess   Yes.

Spectator One   We're just looking out for you.

The **Spectators** *all nod. Some of the Lovers nod, convinced.*

We move straight into –

Part Four: The Break-Up/Down

Everyone is in position for the Partner swap, a little panicked. Partner poses.

Spectator One   Andy and Jess, do either of you want to swap Partners?

They both shake their heads. They look at each other, shaking their heads. They gasp in relief.

Andy (*true*)   Omigod I've never been so happy.

Jess (*true*)   Me too. I'm so glad I found you.

They high ten. **Hayley** *watches forlornly.*

Spectator One   Ella and Jacob, do either of you want to –

Jacob   NO.

Ella   All right then – no.

He wraps his arm around **Ella**. *She receives it, gratefully.*

Ella   Thank you.

Jacob   I love you.

Ella   Thank you. For doing that.

She kisses him on the cheek. **Hayley** *watches forlornly.*

Spectator One   Sam and Max. Do either of you want a new Partner?

Max   No, we don't.

Sam F   Actually, I do. I want Sam to be my Partner.

The **Spectators** *outside cheer.* **Hayley** *gasps, holding onto* **Sam M**.

Spectator   FINALLY

Spectator   I *knew* they were into each other

Spectator   Ring the bells! Love is real!

All Spectators   SAM SQUARED SAM SQUARED SAM SQUARED –

Spectator One   Wait. Are you saying you Love Sam?

Sam F   I'm saying – we're friends. And I'd much rather be partnered with a friend than –

Spectator   Um, that's not allowed

Spectator (*referring to* **Sam M**)   Nooo he's been friendzoned! Look at his sad little friendzoned face

Spectator One   You can't be Partners with someone unless you Love them. Do you Love him?

Sam M *tries not to be too interested in her answer.*

Sam F *is aggravated, unsure what to say.*

Sam F   He's my friend! Is that not enough?

Sam M *is secretly hurt.*

Jess   No. This is *Love*. This is serious. This is the stuff you build a life on. So – do you?

Max *jumps in –*

Max   Wait, Sam. Please. Don't send me Out.

Sam F   You'll be fine. As you've told me, several times, all the girls will be lining up to be your Partner.

Max   But I don't want to try to Love them. I want to try to Love *you*.

Sam F (*sarcastic*)   Wow, I'm convinced.

Max   Look can we just have, like, ten seconds alone, to talk?

Spectator One (*sympathetic*)   Aw.

A brief pause.

Spectator One   Nope!

Max   Fine. If we can't do this in private then –

He takes a deep breath.

I know it's like. Mental or whatever for me to say this, and we haven't known each other that long, and there are so many girls here who are so much more attractive than you but – *sorry* – old habit – listen you've sort of. Got in my head a bit. I think I like you. Like. I don't know what's going on. Like in my body. Like I have no idea what the fuck is going on in my body.

Sam F   Are you serious?

Max   Would I say that lame shit if I didn't mean it? Sorry. Again. I'm trying to stop being a dickhead and start being a little nerd boy like you – *sorry* – I am sorry – I'm trying. Please. Just give me a chance. Just don't send me Out yet.

Sam F *is totally torn. She struggles.*

Sam M   It's okay, Sam, hey, you don't owe me anything. We're here to find Love. You've got to put that first.

Hayley *scowls. They are still linking arms.*

Sam F   I don't know what I'm supposed to do.

Spectator One *steps in –*

Spectator One (*strong*)   Boy Sam, what about you in all this? Do you want to swap Partners?

Sam M   No.

Spectator One   And Hayley?

Hayley   Yes.

A gasp from the Lovers. They are outraged, terrified. **Sam F** *steps forward, instinctively, protectively, towards* **Sam M**.

The **Spectators** *erupt –*

Spectator   THANK THE SWEET BABY JESUS FOR THAT

Spectator   FINALLY, SOME ACTION

Spectator   THANK YOU, Hayley

Spectator   I WAS ABOUT TO GO OUTSIDE OR SOMETHING

Sam M   Hayley? What are you doing?

Hayley   What did you expect, Sam?
I'm just doing it to you before you do it to me.

Sam M   You don't know I was gonna do that.

Hayley   Weren't you?

Sam M *doesn't say anything.*

Hayley   Right. So. I'm supposed to just . . . let you?

Sam M *doesn't say anything.*

Hayley   Exactly. I'm not gonna be left on a sinking ship when the violins are playing. I'm getting in a frigging lifeboat.

Sam M *looks at the ground.*

Hayley   Sorry, Sam. Love youuu.
But crucially, I don't.

She looks around at the other boys.

Hayley   I want to Partner with . . .

Spectator   Lock up your sons, huns. Hayley's on the manpage

Hayley   . . . Andy. I think he needs it the most.

Jess   NO!

Andy   What?

Jess *clutches him tighter.*

Jess   No. You can't leave me.

Spectator   Ooh she's gonna push him way if she squeezes too hard

Andy   I didn't say I was leaving you!

Jess   You're thinking about it though, aren't you?

Spectator   He's THINKING ABOUT IT

Spectator   What a snake

Spectator   Capital F Fuckboy

Jacob (*to* **Ella**)   I'd *never* do that to you.

Andy   I'm not *doing* anything! I don't want to be her Partner!

Jacob   Never in a million years would I –

Hayley   Actually, actually, I choose Jacob.

Another gasp, from everyone.

Spectator   Omigod this is heterosexual carnage.

Everyone stares at **Jacob**.

He looks around, a little lost.

Jacob   Who, me?

He pauses.

Really?

Sam F   Why are you doing this, Hayley?

Hayley   I have my reasons. I don't judge your shit decisions.

Sam F   Yes – you do!

Hayley   Come on, poppet.

Jacob *tentatively walks across the circle to* **Hayley**. **Ella** *is weirdly calm; she always expected this.*

Jacob   Do I just stand next to Hayley, then?

Ella   Well, this is about the most unoriginal thing that's ever happened.

Jacob   She picked me. It wasn't my idea!

Hayley   Pretty easy trade though, wasn't it, Jacob?

Ella (*laughing, given up*)   Give it a rest, Hayley. The war's over.

Jacob (*to* **Ella**)   In my defence. You *weren't* very affectionate. I don't mean to be a prick, but. Kind of feel like you brought this on yourself?

Hayley   Yeah. Sad times.

Ella   Piss *off*, Hayley!

Jacob   Omigod. Have I got two girls fighting over me?

Ella   Wow.

Jacob   Wait –

He rubs his armpits.

Bone dry.
Am I, like, cured?

He puts his arm round **Hayley**.

Jacob   Is this what being a stud feels like?
Why did no one tell me this earlier? Just be a prick and the girls come running. Am I right, Max?

Max   What?

Jacob   Can you girls, maybe, fight a bit more? Like. Fight fight fight?

Hayley *is looking at* **Jacob**, *disturbed.*

Hayley   Actually actually I want Sam again.

Jacob   Shit.

She immediately unhands herself from under **Jacob**'*s arm.*

Hayley (*to* **Sam M**)   You coming back to me, boo?

Sam M   Well, I haven't got much of a fucking choice, have I?

He trudges back to **Hayley**.

Hayley   Awwh.

She does a heart pose with her hands.

Jacob *runs back to* **Ella**, *arms wide.*

Jacob   Ella! I can be with you again! Yay!

Ella   Yay!

She opens her arms. Then smacks him in the face.

Jacob   Shit!
Come on. You've got to forgive me.

Ella   No, I don't.

Jacob   Well, I don't mean to be a prick but –

Ella   Yeah just saying you don't mean to be a prick doesn't automatically save you from sounding like a massive –

Jacob   Well. I'm the only prick you've got. Beggars can't be choosers.

Jess   Wow. New Jacob really *is* a prick.

Spectator   Is anyone else weirdly attracted to him now?

Spectator   Ssh! Magic is happening!

Ella   I'm definitely not choosing you.

Jacob   What are you gonna do then? Do any of you want her?

No one answers. **Ella** *is quite calm.*

Ella   No. I'm choosing no one. I'm choosing to be done.

Jacob   You can't.

Ella   I suspected this wasn't for me and it's not. I don't believe in it. I don't believe in any of this (*she gestures to the circle*).

The ground shakes a very small amount. Everyone stumbles very slightly.

Andy   What was that?

Spectator 1   Wait –

Jacob   She's bluffing

Spectator 1   Wait, don't –

Ella   I'd rather be Out. So I am.

Jacob   What?

Ella *is shot. She is Out. She falls to the floor.*

Jacob *stares in horror.* **Sam F** *shrieks.* **Hayley** *covers her face.*

Spectator One   Shit.

Jacob *desperately looks around the circle.*

Jacob   No. No, wait.

He appeals to his fellow Lovers.

Jacob   Someone.
Someone – love me. Please. Someone just love me. Someone. Love me. I tried so hard! I did what everyone said! I did what I thought everyone wanted! Someone's got to love me. SOMEONE. SOMEONE. SOMEONE'S GOT TO LOVE ME!

He is shot. He's Out. He falls to the floor.

A stunned silence.

Everyone turns to **Spectator One**, *who is staring at the space where* **Jacob**'s *living head used to be.*

Jess (*quietly*)   What do we do now?

After a moment, the **Spectator** *remembers where they are –*

Spectator One (*dazed*)   Sorry – I just completely, briefly, forgot where I was or what I was doing or why then. Just very briefly, I was a little tiny bird, flying high above this moment, you were all so small, and I was so far away, and the wind was whipping around my little arms, my feathers, and the rain was wetting my little tiny bird face, and I was going somewhere else, somewhere far away, somewhere where I could be alone. And sleep.

A pause as everyone stares at them as they stand, staring blankly into space.

Spectator One *suddenly lies on the floor, spent.*

No one immediately knows what to do.

Sam F   Omigod, we have to get out of here.

She starts banging on the circle.

Spectator   Is anyone just starting to find this a bit – depressing?

Spectator   Yeah

Spectator   I just wanted to believe in Love. This just makes me want to see other people

The **Spectators** *one by one start to turn around.*

The ground shakes a little. Everyone stumbles about a bit.

Andy   Serious, what was that?

Sam F *has a brainwave.*

Sam F   Guys. I've got it. I know my answer. Someone ask me the question. I know who I want to Partner with.

Sam M   You do?

Andy   Why are you still playing?

Jess   Are we still playing?

Hayley   Of course we're still playing. We have to keep playing!

Sam F   I don't care about the game. I don't care what happens to me. Just – someone – ask me the question.

No one does.

Sam F   Fine. 'Do you want to swap Partners?'
Yes!
I want to Partner with Sam.

Sam M (*delighted*)   Really?

Hayley   Fucking knew it.

Jess   Well, duh.

Sam F   No! Me. Girl Sam.
I want to Partner with – myself.

Sam M   Wait, what?

An earthquake hits. Everyone falls on the floor, starts to get up again in confusion as –

Hayley   What happened there?

Sam F *runs to the edge of the circle. She puts her hand through.*

Jess   Whoooooahhh.

Andy   Is it like – broken?

Sam F   Are we free?

Jess *goes to touch it, but recoils instinctively.*

Jess   I'm scared.

Hayley   No! We have to keep playing. What happens now?

She runs over to **Spectator One**, *who is still lying on the floor.*

Hayley   WHAT HAPPENS NOW?

Spectator One *rolls over, uninterested.*

She frantically assembles everyone into their Partners whilst she says –

Hayley   We have to keep playing. We have to keep playing. Someone can still win this. Go Love! Go Love! Goooo Love!

Sam F   Hayley, you can't win. It's over.

Hayley   Yes I know I can't win alone. I need a Partner.

Sam F   It's OVER.

Hayley   Can't win without a Partner. That's insane. No one on their own is winning, let's face it. I'd like to Partner with – MAX.

Sam F   What?

Max   *What?*

She grabs **Max** *and starts assembling herself and him into a Partner pose.*

He is shocked, but lets her.

Sam F   What are you doing?

Max (*suddenly bold, bitter*)   Fine. Yeah. I'm partnering with Hayley. To be honest this was my plan all along. Of course it was my plan all along. I didn't want to be your partner, Sam. We're obviously the winners. Look at us.

Hayley   Aw!

Hayley *and* **Max** *stand together.* **Max** *stares bitterly at* **Sam F** *and* **Sam M**.

Hayley   We look good together, don't we?

Sam M *suddenly runs in front of* **Sam F**, *a human shield, yelling at the unseen overlords.*

Sam M   No. Don't hurt Sam! Don't! Take me instead!

Sam F   Hey, it's okay!

Sam M   No, look, I'm so sorry – I know this isn't Love and I'm not allowed to do Big Gestures but, fuck it, I'm doing my Gesture – and it's fucking Big.

He addresses the overlords, and us.

DID YOU HEAR THAT?
I DON'T CARE IF WE'RE NOT PARTNERS
I DON'T CARE IF SHE DOESN'T LOVE ME
BECAUSE I THINK I LOVE HER
AND YOU CAN'T BE OUT IF YOU ARE LOVED
AND *I* LOVE HER
I ACTUALLY PROPERLY OH SHIT THIS FEELS A BIT LIKE I'M
RUNNING INTO A WALL AT SPEED AND MAYBE I LIKE IT *LOVE HER*

Sam F   Sam, no –

He looks at her.

Sam M   I don't care if you just want to be friends and if that's all you want then I am happy to be your friend, I would *love* to be your friend, Sam.
This is me. Being your friend.

He holds his arms out, eyes squeezed shut. Ready.

TAKE ME!

Nothing happens.

He opens one eye, then the other.

Wait? What's happening? Why is nothing – happening?

Sam F   I think. We broke it.

She easily steps over the line. **Sam M** *winces, but there's no need. She is safe. She jumps over and back over the line a few times, demonstrating.*

Sam M   Oh shit.

Hayley   That's quite embarrassing, hun. Like I don't think you had to do all that.

Max   Yeah, mate. Tone it down a notch.

Sam M *is ashamed. He can't quite look at* **Sam F**.

Sam F *is staring at him. Unsure what to say.*

The **Spectators** *are starting to turn round, back into the circle.*

Spectator   Omigod. Did anyone see that?

Spectator   I know. That's like the most romantic thing I've ever seen.

Spectator   For God's sake. Why won't someone do that for me?

Spectator   Yeah I just want someone to voluntarily risk their life for me with absolutely no guarantee of reciprocated feelings. Why can't I find that?

Jess *is still staring at the precipice of the circle, willing herself to step over it.*

Jess   We can leave?

Andy   Jess? What are you doing?

Everyone turns to look at them.

Jess   We can just. Leave?

Sam F   Yeah.

Andy *goes over to her, worried. Everyone watches.*

Andy   Jess, don't leave. We don't know what happens if we leave.

Jess   I know.

Andy   Things might get difficult. Life might pull us apart.

Jess   Yeah.

Andy   We might end up alone.

Jess   Yeah.

Andy   At least if we stay here, we know neither of us will end up without a Partner. Ever.

Jess   Yeah.

He takes her hand in his.

Andy   Let's stay. It's much safer.

Suddenly **Jess** *steps over the line on her own. Hand still in his.*

He cries out in agony.

Andy   No!

She looks back at him.

Jess   Maybe we should be brave.

Andy   I'm not brave enough to be brave.

He takes his hand away.

Jess   Maybe we don't know what the future for us is. Maybe that's okay.

Andy   You said you'd be with me for ever.

Jess   Yeah. I *said* that. Was probably quite irresponsible of me. Since I've got no idea what for ever looks like.

Andy   Are you breaking up with me?

Jess   No!

Andy   Are you future-breaking up with me?

Jess   Well, we might break up! One day! We might not!

Andy   I can't handle the uncertainty.

Jess   I love you, *now*. I'm your Partner, *now*. That's what I'm saying. Now. We've planned out our whole lives in here. Maybe we should go out and – live them instead.

She holds out her hand.

Come on. Be my partner.

He takes it, and steps over the line.

They slowly, hand in hand, walk off stage.

Andy   I'm terrified.

Jess   Me too. Cool, isn't it?

They are gone.

Hayley   Right so, we *must* win now.

Sam F   Fuck's sake Hayley! Who cares? We're going! I'm going.

She start to leave. **Sam M** *is heartbroken.*

Sam M   Sam.
Are you going to leave me hanging? Again?

She turns back to him.

Sam F   Sam.

She thinks. She isn't sure.

Sam F   Come with me.

Sam M   Just tell me. Just tell me how you feel. I need to know.

Sam F   Come with me.

Sam M   I can take it. Whatever you decide, I'll accept it. Just, please, tell me how you feel.

Now the circle wall is broken, The **Spectators** *move into it and around* **Sam F** *and* **Sam M** *as they wish.*

Spectator   God. He's not giving up is he?

Spectator   *This* is the dedication we've been waiting for!

Spectator   *This* is like. *Love.* Isn't it?

Spectator   Proper love. Proper I will embarrass myself several times in a row just because I need to tell you how I feel Love

Sam M   Thanks, guys.

Spectator   Even if it's *really* embarrassing

Sam M   Yep, thank you.

Spectator   What's she gonna do?

Sam F   Um.

Spectator   She can't reject him now

Spectator   No sorry if she does that I'll lose all respect for her

Sam F   I, um –

Spectator   Come on. Tell him you love him back. Tell him. Tell him. It'll be sooo perfect –

Sam F   Wow it's really distracting with everyone, um –

Max   Fuck's sake, do you Love him, Sam?

Sam F   I.

I mean I *like* him, I want to hang out with him, I am reasonably invested in the idea of him not dying, yes I'm pretty on board with the idea of him staying alive, I want him to be happy, and like, have a good time, like, most of the time, I want him to be healthy and fulfilled and have like, thirty minutes of laughter a day and pudding, if he wants pudding, and like, all the vitamins he needs and, like, a good mattress to sleep on and, like, the use of all his limbs, and, y'know for all his dreams to come true and shit. Yeah. Like. That. So what does that mean. Does that mean I . . .

Spectator (*to the overlords*)   Can we help her along, please?

Some romantic music begins to play. Lighting dips, perhaps.

Everyone watches with bated breath. Even **Spectator One** *sits up and watches.*

Sam F   Okay. Yeah. I love him. I . . . love you, Boy Sam.

They come together and hold hands. **Sam F** *is still a bit bamboozled but she does her best to cover it.*

Sam M   I love you, Girl Sam.

They hug.

Everyone left cheers (apart from **Max** *and* **Hayley***, who are privately furious).*

He whispers to her.

Sam M (*whispering*)   That was so good. You nailed it.

Sam F (*confused, not hearing*)   What?

Spectator One *gets up, suddenly enlivened.*

Spectator One   Guys. I dunno about you but . . . Go Love?

Everyone except **Sam F** *cheers –*

All   GOOOO LOVE!

Spectator One *fist pumps the air.*

Spectator One   We are *back*, people! Love really *does* conquer all!

The **Spectators** *excitedly return to their places outside the circle, watching.* **Max** *and* **Hayley** *assemble in their Partner pose, very easily slipping into each other's arms.*

Spectator   Omigod this is so exciting

Spectator   HELLA INVESTED OVER HERE

Sam F   Wait, we can still get out, right?

Sam F *tries the edge of the circle. It's still broken. Everyone's just happily pretending –*

Spectator One (*jolly*)   We'll all still play along if you will! Go Love!

All   GOOO LOVE!

Sam F *starts to pull* **Sam M** *out of the circle by his hand.*

Sam F (*excited*)   Sam! We can still get out! Let's go!

He tugs her back.

Sam M   Why would you want to be Out, now?

Spectator One   Sorry, what was that? Go Love?

All   GOOOO LOVE!

Sam F   Come on! We can go and live our lives! We don't need this any more!

Sam M   Yeah I know, but.
(*Covertly.*) We could still win this.

Sam F (*disbelief*)   What?

Sam M   Come on. If we stay. We'll definitely win.

Spectator One   Go Love?

All   GOOOO LOVE!

He starts assembling a horrified **Sam F** *into a Partner pose with him.*

Sam F   I don't care if we / win.

Sam M (*covertly, smiling*)   Shh. They love us. Our Love is about to, like, *win* at love.

Sam F   But –

Sam M   Shh. Come on. Don't lose this for us.

She looks at **Sam M***, horrified.*

Spectator   There *is* hope for all of us

Spectator   I *knew* Love would conquer all

Spectator (*one hand, the other, together*)   Humanity, faith, restored

Hayley (*to* **Max**)   Smile for God's sake. We can still win this.

Max (*smiling*)   We've lost. I've lost.

Spectator One   I think we all know who's won at love. But since we're still playing –

Spectator   Sam Squared. Best winners ever

Spectator   SOULMATES

Sam M   Come on. Smile. They're choosing the winners.

Spectator One   I guess I *have* to ask the question. Does anyone want to swap Partners?

Sam F   Um –

Sam M (*hard*)   You said you loved me.

Sam F *is taken aback.*

Spectator One   Right, in that case –

Sam F   Actually –

Sam M   Don't you?

She looks at him.

Sam F   Not like this.

She steps forward.

I do.

Spectator One   What?

Sam M   Sam –

Sam F   I want to swap Partners.

Gasps from the **Spectators***.*

Spectator   Wait, what's happening?

Sam M *steps forward, alone.*

Sam M   No, *I* want to swap Partners.

Spectator   No! Go Love! Go Love?

Sam F   I don't want a Partner. I quit. I am Out.

She is shot. She is Out. She falls to the floor.

Sam M   No!

Max   NO!

Hayley *holds* **Max** *upright, to stop him falling to the floor in grief and agony.*

A brief pause.

Sam M   Wait, what happens to –

He is shot. He is Out. He falls to the floor.

A stunned silence.

The **Spectators** *cover their faces, fall to their knees, turn away. They can't watch.*

The **Spectators** *and* **Spectator One** *start to leave, or turn away, during the next.*

Hayley *starts tapping* **Max***, who has covered his face, devastated.*

Hayley   Max, Max. Look. We're the last ones left.

Max   What?

He looks around. She is breathless.

Hayley   I think we won. Omigod, we've won.

Max *steels himself. Rubs his face. Pumps a fist.*

Hayley   Omigod!

She starts jumping up and down, clapping.

Max (*to himself*)   I knew I'd win. I knew I'd win.

Hayley   We won! We won! Go Love! Go Love!

They are alone on stage.

Hayley and Max   GOOOO LOVE!

Lights fall, immediately.

End of play.

Find a Partner!

BY MIRIAM BATTYE

Summary of a recorded conversation between Find a Partner! *writer Miriam Battye and director Matt Harrison.*

Miriam, originally from Manchester, has been a writer for ten years. She started out working with young people, community groups, children – lots of large casts. She has always had a dream to write for Connections. Her latest play *Scenes with girls* premiered at the Royal Court Theatre in February 2020.

The play originated from Miriam's love of reality TV, and her wish to understand why we love it. Lots of reality TV exposes people's anxiety around coupling – the need to do it quickly and in public and being judged on those choices, which happens in real life too. She took these elements and built a story around it.

The play isn't about reality TV. It's about the things that surround it, and how it mirrors real life. The world and tone of the play is heightened. It is life turned up to 100.

The idea behind the contestants being shot when they are out of the game was to make the pressure of finding love extreme – if you fail you cease to exist, cease to matter.

The characters are archetypes, 'the hurt one', 'the hot one', 'the megalomaniac', etc. Miriam takes these big, vibrant characters and puts them into a ring to see what happens. Everyone knows versions of these characters in real life. This play allows young actors the challenge of hitting those big characters without losing the truth of them, alongside moments of delicacy and smallness.

The Spectators are people with real emotions. Their energy and cruelty comes from them wanting to have an opinion.

The world of this play exists on its own, the play is its own universe. It's an open invitation for companies to create what they want as long as that world feels true.

The moment when the circle breaks, the earthquake, shows the fragility of society and societal rules. If someone says 'I do not want to do this anymore' it has a massive impact.

Within the relationships, it's up to the company to decide whether they are actually 'in love', but that in all the couples there is a real *possibility* of love.

The play was written to explore and expose the ideas of heteronormative relationships, but that's not to say that that can't be subverted. There is a world where genders are swapped or it's a generally bisexual world; it's open to interpretation but make sure to interrogate why you are making your choices.

Miriam invites companies to bring themselves to the play and explore how they can inform the world of the play and what it means.

There are two solid things in this play:

1 It needs to be simple – a circle, possibly with different levels. It is important there are two distinct spaces – one for contestants and one for Spectators.

2 The shot, when people are out of the game, needs to be swift, final and scary. How that is achieved theatrically is up to individual companies.

This is a play about connection. It gives companies the chance to be energetic, playful and theatrical, to really explore what it means to be human.

The hope is that this play will get people talking about commitment, whether romantic or in friendships, and how hard it is, and that it needs to be nurtured and treasured.

Notes on rehearsal and staging, drawn from a workshop with the writer, held on Zoom in November 2020

How Miriam came to write the play

Miriam told her mum that she was writing a play for Connections and her mum said, 'Can you not write one of your nasty plays – can you write a play about love?' She had a strong reaction to that, saying that, 'Love is not nice, it's more like *The Hunger Games*!' She sees love as competitive and divisive and she didn't willingly enter into it.

When she was young she wondered where that desire to love and be loved came from. She wanted to explore the idea that love is so much more than two people just getting on and liking each other; there is so much more that surrounds that point of contact between two people. So she just put some people in a space and pushed that to the extreme.

She has a real love for and fascination with reality television and was a fan of *Love Island* back at the beginning when it was *Celebrity Love Island*. The play has evolved from that. It's definitely not *Love Island* but has evolved from a world where a show like *Love Island* is essential viewing. But this isn't a play about reality TV; it's a play about the world.

Ice breaker

Matt Harrison, the lead director, started the session by going round the whole group and asking them what their name was, where they were joining from and something that they had achieved in the last twenty-four hours that they were proud of, big or small.

When working with young people, this exercise can be important in terms of holding the room, but also starts to shape the questions and feelings that you want to put into the space. Another potential question/provocation to ask your group in these check-in sessions could be: When have you felt an emotion at its fullest?

Questions like this give the opportunity for the company to open up and share things that might be useful within the process.

Exercise: Thinking about the play

In breakout rooms, Matt asked one group to think about PLOT, one to think about CHARACTERS, one to think about WORLD and one to think about the MESSAGE/ HEART of the play:

PLOT – the narrative arc, the core plot points, what has stayed with you?

CHARACTER – what has landed with you about these characters, about their core relationships, who they are as people, what sort of size and tone of character are they?

WORLD – think about the world the story sits in, how does the world feel, what are some of the rules of this world, what are the major players or powers in this world?

MESSAGE/HEART – what is at the heart of this piece, what are the big issues or themes that drive it, what do you think an audience might take away, or some of the questions they might leave with?

Each group then shared their thoughts:

Group 1 – PLOT

- It has a fairly straightforward narrative.
- Main feature – the lovers/contestants are in peril – if they don't succeed in their task they are going to get shot/cancelled. It's a very real threat.
- The ending needs to be straightforward/final – it may feel harsh and jarring but needs to not be sugar coated.
- Spectators and contestants are one – reminiscent of *The Hunger Games*.
- Has a resonance with current 'cancel culture'.

Group 2 – CHARACTER

- They are all fairly two-dimensional character tropes – but the more they speak the more truth there is in what they say and depth to them.
- We judge them – taking things at face value.
- The Spectators are both literally looking down on the contestants like in *The Hunger Games* or *Gladiator* in the Colosseum but also metaphorically; there is a sense of superiority to them.
- The characters are archetypal – we can relate to real people in our own lives.
- Their decision making is quite futuristic. Playing around with sexuality and gender changes them.
- Faceless/nameless men – they set a low benchmark for all the other men in the play that are named, which asks the question: what is the benchmark for masculinity?
- The Spectators are really invested in this game.

It is interesting to look at what happens when you lean into the archetypes – when they feel really useful to hit and when you want to fight to see their vulnerability and realness.

Group 3 – WORLD

- Reminded some of *The Social Dilemma* in Netflix, of someone looking in from behind a screen.
- A focus on the Spectators – they are important too. The lead parts are not necessarily the named characters.
- There is a societal judgement about being worthy only if you find love.
- There is a real emphasis on status.
- The characters don't necessarily know the rules of the world, they don't know what they are, and that mirrors real life.

- Some of the characters understand the rules better than others – what status does that give?
- The performative aspect of this play resonates with real life – dating apps, Instagram, etc.

Group 4 – MESSAGE/HEART

- The shallow and exposing nature of dating.
- Young people are new to the world of dating so might meet this play as observers.
- Everyone's opinion matters.
- The cruelty of the Spectators.
- If you are not in the public eye, you are irrelevant or don't exist – like in *Love Island*, as soon as it's off the screen you forget all about the contestants.
- The immaturity of adults – kids watching *Love Island*, for example, the adult dating world is thrust upon them too early.
- The gamification of dating – Tinder, etc.
- Making assumptions about people and not thinking about the life of the people beyond the show.
- Media being bloodthirsty – only interested in drama.
- If you are on your own you are a loser.
- How important is winning? What is the prize?
- Unpersoned – like in Orwell's *Nineteen Eighty-Four* – the characters in the middle are disposable. As soon as they are shot they are forgotten.
- How does it feel to go from outside to inside the circle, e.g male Sam?
- They never challenge or wonder about the people who have been shot.
- Love is not always sexual – interesting to explore what that means in the context of this play.
- The theme of being shot as soon as you are not 'useful' is interesting to consider – does this have resonance for some people in society more than others?

Ways into the script

1. What is the play's relationship to time and space?

Every story falls into one of the following:

One Space, One Time

One Space, Multiple Times

Multiple Space, One Time

Multiple Space, Multiple Times

Miriam has left it up to the company to decide fully what this relationship is.

It's One Space and it could be One Time, but, and this relates to how you do your transitions (see Q and A with Miriam below), it could be either One Time or Multiple Times, depending on how you interpret the PARTS of the play.

Think about the drive of the play and how tight the arc is. Think about the timescale of the piece. If you think that the play takes place over the course of three days, that is very different to if it takes place over three months or three years. Nail down how much time passes between each 'scene'. Is it only the length of a commercial break? Is it three minutes? Is it a day?

2. Fact and questions

Take a piece of paper and put a line down the middle and title one half FACTS and the other half QUESTIONS.

Then read each scene, as a company, and pick out all the FACTS and all the QUESTIONS. No FACT is too small, e.g names, locations, times, references to gender in the text, references to action, and no QUESTION is too big, e.g the Whys, the Whats, etc.

Two volunteers read p. 16 and the group found the following FACTS:

- There are two people in the scene, Hayley and Joey
- Joey has a normal amount of hair
- Joey has his own teeth
- Hayley is concerned with Joey's physical appearance
- They are currently a couple

The group identified the following questions about the scene:

- Has Joey got something to hide?
- Why is Hayley concerned with Joey's appearance?
- And to what level is she concerned?
- Is Joey telling the truth?
- What has made Hayley value 'Partner Names'?

The facts can be beautiful little things you can cling on to, either for character choices or for choices about the world of the play.

With questions, look to where in the rest of the play you can find the answers. Assume a character is telling the truth unless they are under pressure. If you can't find the answer in the play, that's when you get to make your own choices.

3. Events

You can then dig a layer deeper. You can look at the events in the play and the events in each scene.

The group thought about some of the big events in the whole play and came up with:

- When Sam M switches from saying he loves Sam F to thinking he could win.
- When someone first gets shot.
- When Sam M enters the circle from outside.

Your group may find more/different events. If you mark the events then you know you need to build to these in rehearsal. These are important moments that need to land for an audience.

4. Spacing and punctuation

Punctuation is really important: it controls breath and emotion. It gives the rhythms of the characters' thoughts. Physically it gives the rhythm of when an actor stops breathing and starts breathing.

Exercise: Walk the punctuation

A useful way to get a measure of the rhythms of a speech is to 'Walk the Punctuation' with the company.

The group looked at Jess's speech on p. 9.

Ask the company to walk around the space, saying the speech.

On every full stop – change direction.

On every comma – have a moment of suspension.

On every question mark – clap.

On every ellipsis – a little lean.

On every hyphen – a little bounce.

On every exclamation mark – stomp.

This gives an idea of a character's emotional state, their rhythms of speech and how their thoughts are arriving.

5. Three core questions

There are three questions that are helpful to ask as you begin to create moments, whether in scenes or monologues.

- Why is the character saying these words?
- Who are they speaking to?
- What do they want/need?

Ways into the text with actors on their feet

The group used Max's speech on p. 10 and looked at five different jumping-off points:

Exercise

1 **Positive or negative.** Work through the speech up to every piece of punctuation or even further and think about whether each thought is positive or negative. If positive, then mark a step to the left, and if negative, a step to the right. You can use a click or a smaller movement; what is important is the physicalisation of it.

2 **Antithesis.** Where two different ideas or feelings are placed next to each other. Again, same as above, work through the speech and mark moments of antithesis with either a step or a click or some other movement of your choice.

3 **Earth and sky.** There are moments in a speech that reference what is above us and can reveal what ideals or ideas a character has, e.g. gods, love, etc. There are also things that are more earthy, e.g. lust and desire, things that feel baser, dirtier. Work your way through the speech and mark these moments with a reach up for sky and a reach down for earth.

4 **Pronoun map**. In a speech, just focus on the use of pronouns. Acknowledge the personal Is and Mes, and also the others, the Theys and Thems and also references to the outside world. Work through the speech and physicalise them – really place the Is and Mes on yourself with your hand, really place specifically the Theys and Thems in the space around you, and acknowledge the world beyond with a arching arm gesture.

5 **Landing a piece of text.** Using a post-it note or a piece of paper, on each line (you don't have to write on it) place the paper either on yourself, the person you are speaking to or the space, depending on where the character wants that line to land. Then think about *how* you want that line to land. Slapping the paper down is very different to placing it down gently. If you are speaking to another person, if you want the line to land on someone else, you can start to think about what part of the body you want it to land on. For example, if you want the line to appeal to reason, you could place it on their head, if you want it to land emotionally, you could place it over their heart, if it is something that questions strength, you could place it on the bicep.

One of the participants in the group reflected that it was a really lovely exercise to get their company to think about more than just saying their lines out front; there are other options and this is a nice way to introduce that idea to them.

Conjuring the world, design ideas and theatrical moments

Collect images that reflect, inspire and resonate with the play. Put them up in your rehearsal room either in real life or in your digital room. Interrogate how they make you and the company feel.

Exercise: Images

Matt asked the group to find an image that resonated with them about the play, something that inspired them. It could be anything from a magazine cutting, a line from a book or an image from the internet. He then asked everyone to share their images. As music was played, he asked everyone to flick through all the images and put into the chat box which ones they liked or which resonated with them.

Some examples of images:

- A *Love Island* contestant
- A lady with big 1980s hair
- The quote 'don't grow up, it's a trap'
- The quote 'ME lol why'
- A pepperoni pizza
- Someone at a computer overseeing other people
- Sun newspaper headlines about Caroline Flack
- A cruise ship

Exercise: Provocations

Matt gave the group some provocations. First, he asked everyone to put into the chat the answer to the provocation 'I loved the moment when . . .'

This question is framed as if the show has already been made and you have just watched it. Imagine this is the biggest, boldest version you could have made, what is the moment that resonated most?

Some examples from the group:
I loved the moment when . . .

- the circle was broken
- we had a rotating stage with bright lighting and we could shift the audience's eye-line
- the bodies are piled up in a corner
- Boy Three has been picked
- the songs happen, there is a live band on stage using music to interrupt the scene and remind us of the message/theme
- the ensemble made the theme tune

The next provocation was, 'The play is like . . .' It might be that, for example, 'The play is like a mash-up of this show and that show and that other show' or it might be more tactile, 'The play is like holding a balloon or licking an ice lolly.'

Some examples from the group:
The play is like . . .

- a thunderstorm
- first love on steroids
- a box of chocolates – as you unwrap the layers, you start to see that we are all made of mush

- looking in a mirror
- listening to young people describe dating and being dumped!
- a fluffy pink cloud land
- the current reality for young people
- a broken mirror
- like social media becoming a reality
- like *Love Island* meets *Googlebox* meets *The Hunger Games!*

The next provocation was: What is the project under the play? What do you want your play to say or do?

Some examples from the group:

My project under the play is . . .

- to show what love is being reduced to
- to have a jolly good laugh
- to allow our young people to find their confidence and voice again
- to ask where we went wrong
- to get the students to question how real they are
- to encourage the actors to explore the characters and realise their vulnerabilities
- to give space to young people to explore relationships and give them the room to explore the unconventional
- to show that disabled young people have relationships and to support them to feel comfortable inhabiting dating stories

Further provocations

Matt then talked about some of the questions and provocations he would ask of the play when approaching a text to dig into the world a bit more:

- What is the power hierarchy in the play? Who has the power in this world?
- What are the expected gender principles? What are the male and female expectations in the world? How does that change if you mix up the gender dynamics?
- What are the societal codes in the world? Who speaks when? How do they speak? How do they enter and exit a space?
- Size of the world – is this a world that is quite small or really expansive? How does the size impact things?
- Totems – are there any objects that feel particularly powerful or important?
- What is your play's relationship to the audience? Are they just passive? Are they treated like Spectators? How complicit are the actual audience?

Character

No characters in this play are the same from the beginning to the end. There are clear journeys for some of them, but potentially not for the Spectators. There is hopefully joy for actors playing Spectators to discover their own journey with their character.

A useful exercise could be to ask your actors to draw their character journeys. Mark a point on a piece of paper as the start and one as the end of their journey. Invite them to go through the play in their mind and show the highs and lows and plateaus of their character. It should end up looking like a heartbeat monitor. You can then attach the peaks and troughs to certain events that happen in the play. You can then go further and do the same exercise but with individual scenes.

The best definition of character that Matt has ever heard was from Ken Campbell (an actor, writer and director, well known for experimental theatre and improvisation). He said that:

Character = Choices made under pressure.

Matt suggested giving your actors some character questions to think about. Below are the questions he likes to use, but this is by no means an exhaustive list:

- Name
- Nickname
- Date of birth – links to star signs
- Where were you born?
- Parents and siblings names?
- How would you describe your parents?
- What traits have you inherited?
- What you wanted to be when you were younger and what changed?
- Favourite taste?
- Favourite smell?
- How would you describe your style?
- What do people in the street think of you? How are you perceived?
- On the morning of the speech/scene/play what are you thinking about most?
- What in life makes you happiest?
- What is your biggest fear?
- What is the thing you want the most?
- What is stopping you from achieving this?
- What is a secret about you no one knows?
- What do you have to gain in the speech/scene/play?
- What do you have to lose in the speech/scene/play?

If this gets too intellectual you can do a visualisation exercise with your actors:

- Imagine you are looking at your character through a one-way mirror, like in a police interview. Really take them in. Describe what they are wearing, how recently they have washed, the quality of their haircut, what have they got in their pockets?

Then you can ask your actors to think about the physical lead points of their character.

- Are they led by their chest? Their heart, are they emotional?
- Are they led by their head? Their brain, more cerebral?
- Are they led by their groin? By lust?
- Are they led by their hands? Are they fidgety, do they need to be always doing something?

Then think about what piece of time they sit in. Are they always thinking about the future? What are they aiming for, striving for? Are they sitting in the present, dealing with what's happening right here, right now? Or are they in the past? Are they dealing with trauma and events that happened in the past they can't let go of?

Emotional connection

Exercise: Personal images

It could be useful to ask your actors, 'What skin do you have in the game, what is *your* connection to the character?'

Matt led an exercise where everyone took a piece of paper and drew a grid with six boxes, like a comic strip. The group then looked at Andy's speech on p. 9 and went through the speech, image by image, rather than line by line or thought by thought, and found moments in their own life that resonated. They then distilled these into one image, and drew them in the comic strip.

Matt explained that this exercise is really useful when dealing with the chunky emotional moments and can be good to explore the imagery and feelings it conjures.

If for whatever reason your young people are not comfortable sharing personal experiences, it might be useful to use stories from television or films that are comparable to give that emotional connection some context.

Finding simplicity in the text

Exercise: Talking to a baby

Invite your actors to find something that they can use as a baby, for example a rolled-up jumper or a big plastic bottle. Ask them to do a speech or scene to the baby as if it's theirs. How does this change the way they are saying the lines? How does it feel to strip away all the other context and focus on a sense of intimacy between them and someone they love? Also about the cost, about potentially having to say some not nice things and make someone so young understand why they are behaving in a certain way. This can be a really useful exercise if you find some of your actors being demonstrative and need to pull things back. What might it unlock in the scene that you might not have realised?

Reflections from the group after doing this exercise:

- It felt much more light hearted
- It felt like more of a 'safe' confession
- It brought an unexpected vulnerability

Another useful exercise if actors are stuck on a speech or a moment is to get a tennis ball or small object and get them to throw it between them as they play the scene. This helps to kick them out of any rhythmic habits that they may have got stuck in. Also domestic tasks are great, e.g tying a shoelace, simple repetitive tasks that stop us 'acting'.

Blocking

A good exercise to start to think about the shape of the piece and physically find the world outside of the stage directions is to use viewpoints. Get the company in the space and give them a limited choice of movement, e.g. run, stand, sit, walk and really begin to play with those simple things. Initially let them begin in their own world and then be impacted on by others around them. This can also work well in an online rehearsal scenario – you can then introduce a sense of architecture; for example, how do they use the physical shape and items in the room to affect how they move, such as reaching for a light bulb, or matching their body to the edge of their box on Zoom? You can then introduce copying or mirroring to bring a different dynamic. This exercise may well throw up some interesting shapes or moments that you can use later in the play.

Devising exercise

Matt said he found it useful to set some little devising tasks around moments in the play. Using pages 28 and 29 of the play as a stimulus, and only using one object, three physical moves, one entrance and one exit, tell the story of giving a tour of the space you are in.

Again there might be an image, a moment that sparks something. It may give you the beginning of a movement language for your play.

Question and answer with Miriam Battye

Q: Can we change some of the words, e.g. wanker, to something more regional/native?

A: If you have a sense of what the word wanker means and you can find a word that suits your group more, then absolutely.

Q: What needs to be solid, what feels important to be as it is and where is there flexibility?

A: I don't see it as needing a lot of set, but even that I'm willing to be questioned on.

Q: Can we soften the swear words if a younger cast feels awkward using them?

A: Yes, of course, the actor comes to the text, the language can move to fit them, as well as hopefully them finding things that push them outside of themselves.

Q: What TV season is the show in?

A: Good question. I don't know, have fun! I'm always keen to put the responsibility at the feet of the company as they know their version of the play better than I do. But my instinct is that the world of the play begins at the beginning of the play and ends at the end, there is nothing outside of that. It is similar to real love: we go into it knowing we may get hurt but we do it anyway, because the rewards are massive. I would really encourage you not to worry about this world not being 'possible' in our world.

MH: I think it's right to say that this exists within its own bubble and what that allows is to play the sincerity, simplicity and stakes of the play.

Q: How do you see the transitions between the scenes?

A: I wrote the play to make sense on the page as well, which is why we have Part One, etc. I can see a world where these are announced but I don't think that's necessary. It's up to the company, they are free to do what they want. Transitions are a great place to lay your table out and show how you are commanding the space.

MH: Transitions can help to give a sense of time passing and the physical language of the play. It gives you the chance to show the moving on to the next part of the game show, moving up a level.

Q: If we are rehearsing and performing entirely online, can we play with the televisual aspect even though it's a play?

A. Yes. Even though it was written to be in a theatrical space, in the current times we need to find other 'theatrical spaces'. Just be true to the space you are in. Make a choice and be true to it.

Q: Do you have thoughts on the physical aspect of the play, the hand holding, the kissing, if all rehearsals and performances are online?

A: This is a new frontier. It's about play and seeing what can work.

MH: This is something we are all wrestling with. It's about showing moments of connection. Whether that is through a visual thing of matching up a Zoom background, colours, costume items that they are holding in their own screens. Is it about proximity in the 'Zoom squares'? Or can you use the chat function in an interesting way? With holding hands and kissing emojis? Can you use breakout rooms to create intimacy?

Q: Can we add music to certain parts, e.g as the Spectators say 'GO Love' can they be sung? And can we add additional songs that might fit with new lyrics?

A: Yes to the first one. And no to the other, as it may take away from the story.

Q: With a large cast, can we interject our own Spectator comments?

A: It's a good question. The play operates within its own rhythms, so I'm slightly hesitant to say yes, but in order to create atmosphere you might want to add other noise/words, but be careful it doesn't take the focus away from the text as written.

Q: Do you have ideas about how this play looks different in a city world versus a more rural setting?

A: It's outside the rural or the city, it's its own place, it's heightened. It's just important that there are two distinct spaces, inside and outside the 'circle', and that it can be broken.

Q: How neutral are the Spectators?

A: It's tricky working with an ensemble/chorus. Each line that the Spectators have can be filled with lots of energy and personality, but the danger is if they carry that same energy and personality throughout the whole play, then we lose focus on the story. They are full blooded people, but think about where you want the audience to focus and find the moments of unity in the Spectators.

Q: How much can we pre-record?

A: Do whatever works for you!

Q: How much is the shock of the gun important? Any ideas of alternatives?

A: The 'Out' moments need to be final. They should be big and scary and should be immediate. BANG and they are gone. These moments shouldn't be drawn out. There is a simple version where the people who are 'Out' sit down/leave the space? Maybe using a cymbal or a gong or a bell to give the jolt.

Q: Is double casting ok?

A: I want the piece to function in whatever circumstances you find yourselves in; we need to solve problems creatively. So yes to creative doubling.

Q: Why is Sam F there? Why would she put herself in this position?

A: The world of the play is its own world and operates within its own rules. Sam needs to operate within it and navigate her way through this world to fall in love; this is what is important.

Q: Does the 'shooter' have to be unseen or can it be a seen gunman or perhaps the Spectators?

A: I don't think you should have a cast member doing the shooting – that tells a different story but certainly exploring the savagery of those moments feels really interesting.

A final piece of advice from Miriam:

> Find the energy and the sense of play, don't worry and enjoy it!

Suggested references

Gogglebox
Love Island
Reality TV shows
The Hunger Games
The Social Dilemma (drama-documentary on Netflix)
Nineteen Eighty-Four by George Orwell

From a workshop led by Matt Harrison
with notes by Kash Arshad

Like There's No Tomorrow

created by the Belgrade Young Company with
Justine Themen, Claire Procter and Liz Mytton

There are strange cracks appearing in the land on the other side of the world, turning habitats into wastelands and creating a new wave of climate refugees. However, no one's worrying about that here – where a mayoral candidate is promising more, more, more. New industries, new jobs, new homes and masses of new stuff – all of it achieved by expansive and rapid economic growth. It's what the people want. Apart from Maru that is, whose asthma is really bad because the air is already thick with pollution, and their mantra of reduce, reuse, recycle is falling on deaf ears. Their only sanctuary is the local park. Lush and green, it's where Maru can reconnect, recharge and breathe.

However, as plans emerge to build on the park, and Maru's parents appear to be seduced by the mayoral candidate's invitation to consume as much as you can, something has to give. So, when a crack appears in Maru's new state-of-the-art bedroom furniture and then it spreads to the centre of town, and Maru seems to be the culprit, it's enough to focus everyone's attention – as they seek to deal with the symptom, whilst remaining oblivious of the cause.

Like There's No Tomorrow was created with the Belgrade Young Company, through a process of discussion, research, improvisation, scripting and revision. They first performed this play on 9 March 2020.

Cast size

10–16
plus additional ensemble members

There are eight named characters in the play, and a minimum of two additional company members are required to cover the chorus roles – making a minimum company of ten.

The number of company members playing chorus roles could be increased to eight – making a maximum company of sixteen with reasonable speaking roles. There is also the possibility of including a further eight to twelve company members in non-(or little-)speaking roles, delivering the movement sequences in the city, the scene changes and the bringing to life of the folk tale in Scene Three.

Like There's No Tomorrow was first presented by the Belgrade Young Company at the Belgrade Theatre, Coventry, on 9 March 2020, with the following cast:

Maru	Oluwasemilore Kaji-Hausa
Fin	Femi Themen
Asha	Seyi Olomolaiye
Bobby Brunt	Sachin Sharma
Mum	Ifeolu Olomolaiye
Dad	Tillman Osici
Luca	Emma Gibson
Georgie	Georgie Gibson
Campaigner/Neighbour	Jess Lake
Elder/Journalist	Kimberley Musa
Student/Fly-Tipper	Luqman Mwalim
Campaigner/Fin's Mum	Yolande Thompson

All other parts were played by members of the Company

Director/Devising Facilitator Justine Themen
Co-Director/Devising Facilitator Claire Procter
Assistant Directors Jules Chan, Sebbie Mudhai
Dramaturg Ola Animashawun
Wordsmith Liz Mytton
Songsmith Unamay Olomolaiye
Designer Janet Vaughan
Lighting Designer Adam Warren
Sound Designer Oliver Howard

Justine Themen (Devising Facilitator/Co-Director) is a theatre director and change-maker. She is currently Deputy Artistic Director of the Belgrade Theatre and Co-Artistic Director for its City of Culture 2021 programme. During her time at the Belgrade, she has built a small participatory programme into a broad-reaching ethos across the work of the building. The programme provides access to arts activity to some of the city's least arts-engaged communities, shapes talent development opportunities that strongly promote diversity across the sector and creates new work for the theatre's stages. Her co-created work includes *Rise* (Belgrade Young Company), *Walk for Your Life* (Belgrade Black Youth Theatre), *Hussan and Harry* (Belgrade Youth Theatre with Coventry Refugee Centre) and *The First Time I Saw Snow* (Belgrade Theatre). Directing work focuses on new work from female writers of colour – *Red Snapper* (Liz Mytton), *Under the Umbrella* (Amy Ng), both Belgrade Theatre. Prior to working at the Belgrade, she worked for six years in Senegal and Suriname co-creating theatre (*Hia Maun*, Stiching Botopasi) and documentaries (*Abigail*, VPRO), and using the arts as a tool in development and cultural diplomacy.

Claire Procter (Devising Facilitator/Co-Director) is the Belgrade Theatre's Creative Producer for Education. She has over twenty years experience working with children and young people, both as a class teacher and theatre practitioner. Prior to joining the Belgrade, Claire worked for renowned theatre-in-education (TiE) company Big Brum. She has written and co-created a number of original plays for and with young people, including *The Impossible Language of the Time* (Belgrade Youth Theatre/Chris O'Connell), *Room to* Grow (Belgrade TiE) and *On the Line* (Belgrade Youth Theatre/ Jennifer Farmer). Her work to integrate TiE methodology into the making of the Belgrade's youth theatre work has been central to the development of the theatre's participatory practice.

Liz Mytton (Wordsmith) is a playwright and poet based in the North West. She took part in the Critical Mass writing programme at the Belgrade Theatre in 2014, which led to the production of her first full-length play, *Red Snapper*, a runner-up for the 2016 Alfred Fagon Audience Award. In 2018 as a Bristol Old Vic Open Session writer, Liz wrote *Across the River*, about Marcus Garvey and the KKK, which featured in Bristol Ferment Fortnight. Liz has also developed a piece of work exploring hate crime, *Southside Stories*, which premiered at the Tobacco Factory in February 2019, and recently her own musical project, *Shame Shanties*, which uses seas shanties to explore women's mental health. Liz regularly works as a writer and lyricist with Talking Birds Theatre Company in Coventry, most recently on a commission for the Shakespeare Birthplace Trust. She has worked with the Belgrade's Young Company on two occasions in the role of wordsmith – firstly on *Rise* in 2017, and again in 2020 on *Like There's No Tomorrow*.

The Belgrade Young Company was established to give young people showing particular talent/ability from across the Belgrade's participatory programme an opportunity to grow their skills and abilities in a semi-professional context. Past work has included Frank Wedekind's youth classic *Spring Awakening*, rarely performed by young people of the same age as the characters; a physical production of *The Tempest* with Frantic Assembly; and *Rise*, co-created with a company of ten young women aged thirteen to twenty-three about their experiences of discrimination and rising beyond it.

The Belgrade Theatre has an enviable track record of working in radical ways with young people through theatre. In 1965, it developed the first theatre-in-education company, a company dedicated to using theatrical performance and drama workshops to explore issues of cultural, social, political and moral significance as part of a free service to schools and the young people of Coventry. TiE encouraged children to investigate challenging situations for themselves, to search to find the answer, rather than be given it on a plate. This ethos continues to inform the work of the theatre today.

'We conceived of ourselves as separated from nature, we felt cunning and almighty . . .
We usurped nature, we dominated and wounded it. We incited Prometheus, and buried Pan. So much haughtiness made us lose our sisterhood with the butterflies, the flowers, the trees and the roots. So much outrageous greed made us lose the harmony and the care, the connection and the belonging.'

Alessandro Michele, Creative Director, Gucci
May 2020

Characters

Maru
Parent One *of Maru*
Parent Two *of Maru*
Luca, *Maru's older sibling*
Georgie, *Maru's younger sibling*

Fin, *Maru's best friend*
Bobby Brunt, *campaigning to be Mayor*
Asha, *emerging from the Crack (a singer)*

Community Elder *(a singer)*
Teens One *and* **Two**, *at school with Maru*
Teacher *at Maru's school*
Campaigners One *and* **Two** – *Brunt's team, supporting his campaign*
Neighbours One *and* **Two**
Aide *to Brunt*
New Parent (with baby)
Child *and* **Parent**, *stuck in traffic*
Chancer, *selling T-shirts*
YouTuber, *filming the Crack*
Parkour Youths, *jumping the Crack*
Negative Nelly
Journalist
Camera Person
Pastor
Fly-Tippers One *and* **Two**
Child *and* **Mother**, *escaping the city*
Crowd One, Two, Three *and* **Four**
Village Community/City Dwellers/Storybook Villagers/Children/Crowd
Crack

All characters have gender-neutral names and can be played by performers of any gender. Pronouns used in the script reflect the gender of the original Company and can be adjusted accordingly.

Thanks to Frances Marks for making it possible to put on a production of the play as part of the development process for the final script.

Note from the Company

This play was devised by the Belgrade Young Company between October 2019 and March 2020. The basic narrative of human beings failing to live well with the natural world, with a global crisis as the inevitable consequence, was conceived before the outbreak of COVID-19 – as was the narrative of an inability to breathe being a direct impact of climate change on humans beings, and global leaders seeing rescuing the economy as the only way out. As we filled in the details, of course, we were influenced by events happening around us, able to draw on real-life responses to the unfolding COVID crisis as we scripted and improvised our story. The show was first performed on 9 March 2020, with the run ending on Saturday 14 March, the last day of performances before the Belgrade Theatre closed to the public in response to the government announcement that people should avoid attending theatres. All through the week of performances, audiences asked us how we had managed to foreshadow so closely the circumstances of the pandemic. Our answer is twofold. Firstly, the world is 'knowable': evidence is out there for all who choose to listen that the resources of the earth are finite, and that our constant draw on them is creating crisis on a massive scale that may eventually end our very existence; so we are not saying anything that has not been spoken now for decades, but which fails to be heard by Western leaders with their heads in the sands of the myth of eternal economic growth – we are simply listening and finding the truth in both the global and our personal narratives. Secondly, the joys of devising and of working over a longer period of time (as is usually the way with youth theatres) include the ability to draw on material influenced by the world around us right up to the last moments before performance – Trump, Johnson, politicians, campaigners, friends, parents are all in there, feeding the words of our characters, the situations they find themselves in. And in working with young people, too, the drive is to be responsive, to want to make change in the real world. We hope that you find both the personal and the global resonances and help us to continue to spread the urgent messages of the current climate crisis.

Performance Notes

Central to this play is the relationship between capitalism and environmental decline, with a focus on the tension between the West and the developing world. During our process, we chose to locate part of our story in Zimbabwe as this reflected the origins of some of our company members, but there is flexibility in this – future companies may choose another country in place of Zimbabwe and amend elements of the text accordingly (the Shona language used in the Prologue and by Asha in Scene Ten; the story in Scene Three; Asha's narrative about the substitution of crops for tobacco in Scene Ten). This is entirely feasible provided the story reflects the truth of communities at risk of environmental damage and disaster.

Wherever possible, it is our intention for the action to flow seamlessly from one location and one scene to the next. These transitions are marked in bold text – and either described or denoted by the stage direction *'Into'*.

Prologue: Balance

We are part of a community, a community of warmth, generosity and light. The scene is rich with colour and rhythms and the air is thick with expectation.

The community sings a ritual libation giving thanks to Mother Earth. The ritual is led by a **Community Elder** *and supported by a child,* **Asha***. The* **Elder** *carries some water in a calabash, and one of the* **Villagers** *wafts some incense amongst the crowd. The* **Elder** *pours a portion of the water with each verse, showing* **Asha** *how to pour. By the end of the song, the* **Elder** *hands over to* **Asha** *to pour.*

The audience need to be captivated, so that when this world is gone, they too feel the loss.

Elder   Great Mother!

Community   Great Mother! We thank you, Great Mother!

Elder   You, who with loving hands, sculpts the clay from your earthy womb

Community   Form us!

Elder   Who, from your verdant sanctuary, yield both root and fruit

Community   Feed us!

Elder   Who, in your ancient wisdom, sends both storm and flower

Community   Teach us!

Elder   Who, with graceful force, forges rocks and continents

Community   Shield us!

All (*singing*)
    You are the Mother, we are the children,
    Hear our prayer!
    Ndini mai vacho, isu tiri vana
    Hear our prayer!

Elder   To those who came before
Those who lit our way
Let us honour your memory
Let us carry your stories.

(*Singing.*)
    You are the Mother . . .

Community
    . . . we are the children,
    Hear our prayer!
    Ndini mai vacho, isu tiri vana
    Hear our prayer!

Elder   For we who are blessed to be here and now
May we be mindful of our legacy

Consider those who are yet to come
And tend the gardens of tomorrow

(*Singing.*)
    You are the Mother . . .

Community
    . . . we are the children,
    Hear our prayer!
    Ndini mai vacho, isu tiri vana
    Hear our prayer!

Asha   For the children of our future
We pray you have the confidence
To stand strong in the gale
But yet the humility to bend in the breeze

(*Singing.*)
    You are the Mother . . .

Community
    . . . we are the children,
    Hear our prayer
    Ndini mai vacho, isu tiri vana
    Hear our prayer!

The singing draws to an end. Through the smoke of the libation comes the reality of the toxic air of a city, a perversion of the tendrils of the incense.

Into:

Scene One: City

This is the same earth, but what is different is us. Through a movement sequence, we see that we have the power to transform something that is beautiful into something that is destructive. Earth's resources have become a commodity, the balance has tipped. We no longer live for the meaningful, but for the material.

We see the people of the city driving cars, being wasteful with our resources, polluting our world with chemicals, rushing from one place to the next with no time for reflection.

The pollution that we pump into the air is also taken into the air we breathe. The inhabitants of the city struggle to catch a breath. They struggle to breathe in chorus. They are straining, reaching for a lungful of clean air . . .

The city clears into a school scene.

Some **Teens** *are walking into a school classroom, one holding a textbook.* **Maru** *is sat reading a book. There are two bins – an ordinary bin and a recycling bin.*

Teen One   I'm so tired of being treated like a machine!

Teen Two (*turning the pages of her textbook*)   Yeah! How can we answer all these questions by tomorrow?

Teen One *suddenly reaches over and tears the pages out of the textbook.* **Maru** *notices and winces.*

Teen Two What are you doing?!

Teen One *screws the paper into a ball and points at the bin.*

Teen One Solving all our problems!

Teen Two Bet you can't!

Teen One Watch me!

Teen Two Okay . . .

Teen One *throws a piece of paper, and misses the target.*

Teen Two (*laughing*) What was that?!

Teen One You try then!

Teen Two *tears more pages from the book.* **Maru** *pointedly moves her chair away from the* **Teens**, *banging it on the floor.*

Teen Two You need to try and get a bit of a flick into it. Now watch!

Teen Two *aims more specifically, making the sound of the 'flick' to give focus, but still misses.*

Teen One (*laughing*) It's all the way over there! The bin's here!

Maru *disapproves.*

Teen Two You try again!

Teen One (*pulling back to take aim, and so getting closer to* **Maru**) Let me try to get a 'flick' into it!

They are laughing louder now. **Teen One** *misses again.*

Maru What are you doing? Tearing up a textbook is one thing, but you're not even throwing the paper in the recycling bin! I mean it's literally just there!

Teen One It's a game.

Teen Two Yeah, calm down, Maru!

Maru But, why would you . . .?

The **Teens** *ignore* **Maru**. *A low groaning sound can be heard by the audience, but not by the* **Teens**. **Maru** *senses it as unease, rather than as a sound that can be heard. It lasts until* **Maru** *asks them to stop again.*

Teen Two I'm gonna film it.

Teen One Go on then.

Teen Two Five pounds that it won't go in.

Teen One Alright, a fiver!

Teen One *throws and it goes in.*

Told you!

Teen One *dances a victory dance, with* **Teen Two** *filming. They are laughing and jostling, while* **Maru** *eyes them disapprovingly, shaking her head.*

Teen Two   What?!

Maru   Look at all the paper on the floor!

Teen One   What don't you get about having fun?

Maru   What don't you get about not wasting paper? Are you fuckin' stupid?

Teen Two   What? What did you call me?

Teen One   She called you fuckin' stupid! Don't have it!

The **Teens** *'square up', ready to fight, and* **Maru** *jostles with them to get out of their way.* **Teacher** *approaches.*

Teacher   Excuse me!

Teen One   Miss, Maru tried to hit us!

Teen Two   Yeah, she started shouting and 'effing' at us for no reason!

Maru   Miss, I did not! Look at the paper all over the floor!

Teacher   Maru, we do not tolerate swearing in this school!

Maru   I was just reading! And they were ripping up a book – destroying school property – then throwing paper all over the floor!

The **Teens** *stand behind the* **Teacher** *imitating her.*

Teacher   And I will deal with them later. But swearing is completely unacceptable.

Maru (*coughing*)   But, miss –

Teacher   Enough, Maru! (*To* **Teens**.) Don't you have a class to go to?

Teen One *and* **Teen Two** *leave, looking smug.* **Maru** *is angry, and is coughing heavily.*

Maru *notices a* **Crack** *on the floor/wall, as does the* **Teacher**.

Teacher   Where did that come from? What on earth have you been getting up to?

Maru   Nothing. Maybe it was the class before us. (*Coughing.*)

Teacher   Are you okay? Do you need some water?

Maru   No. I'll use my inhaler. (*Looking in bag, but not finding it.*) I'll be fine.

Teacher   Good. And Maru, I'm disappointed in your behaviour.

Teacher *hands* **Maru** *a slip of paper.* **Maru** *reads it – it is a detention slip.*

Teacher   I'll see you in detention on Monday.

Maru *and* **Teacher** *go in opposite directions, with* **Maru** *looking back at the* **Crack** *suspiciously.*

The city crosses through the space, clearing the school and leaving the Mayoral **Campaigners** *in the city centre, handing out flyers. They try to attract the attention of passers-by, drawing them into conversation where they can.*

Campaigner One   Vote Bobby Brunt for Mayor.

Campaigner Two   Hi . . . hi . . . vote Bobby Brunt. Thank you.

Campaigner One   Bobby Brunt for Metro Mayor. Here, if I could just give you . . . (*Hands over a flyer.*)

Campaigner Two   Bringing car manufacturing back to the city. Yes, you heard right, your ears did not deceive you! Bobby's going to open the factories and get us all working again!

Maru *and* **Fin** *enter. They're busy laughing at something on* **Fin***'s mobile phone.* **Campaigner One** *walks in front of them, trying to hand a flyer to a passing shopper, causing* **Fin** *and* **Maru** *to stop in their tracks.*

Campaigner One   End to the proposed congestion zone. Free access to the city centre for all.

Campaigner Two   Nice jacket, madam. I bet you'd be interested to hear about our exciting new plans for the shopping centre . . . the world's biggest Trimark!

Campaigner One   The proposed Green Park housing development will create one hundred and forty-two new homes for families moving into the city by . . .

Fin   What?

Campaigner One   Excuse me?

Fin   You just said they're building on Green Park . . .

Campaigner One   Oh . . . (*Beat.*) Here, take one of these for your parents. (*Handing over flyers.*) It's all in there . . . (*Returning to previous conversation.*) By utilising green space in prime development locations right here in the city centre –

Maru   You want to build on our park?

Campaigner Two   Well, it's everyone's park, not just yours. It's our plan to invest in local infrastructure –

Fin   You can't do that!

Campaigner Two   Let the people decide, eh? It's called democracy. (*Patronisingly.*) Parks are expensive things to run. Where's all the money coming from?

Maru   But where will we go after school? (**Maru** *is starting to cough.*)

Fin   And where's my mum going to walk our dog?

Maru   And what about the music festival?

Campaigner Two   Money doesn't grow on trees, you know. Which is why we need to cut them down and replace them with something that generates wealth. Breathing life back into the city.

Campaigner One (*reading from the flyer*)   'By investing in new homes we're making the city centre a more attractive place in which to live.' (*Points to the flyer.*) See? Nice houses attract nice people, producing a tidy profit.

Fin   But there's no other park for miles –

Campaigner Two   You've got to see the bigger picture here. A housing development really is a win-win for everyone.

Campaigner One (*placating them*)   Why don't you have a pen? Here, take two. (*Hands the pens to* **Fin**.) Nearly forgot, pen for your friend! (*To* **Campaigner Two**.) Kids love pens. (*To* **Maru** *and* **Fin**.) Now if you don't mind . . . (*Awkward beat before* **Campaigner One** *moves off.*) Hello, sir, have you got a minute? I'd like to tell you about Bobby Brunt's stance on immigration . . .

Campaigner Two   Vote Bobby Brunt for Mayor!

The **Campaigners** *continue their mission to engage passers-by, leaving* **Fin** *and the coughing* **Maru** *alone, looking at their gifts.*

Maru   Well, that sucks.

Fin   Come on, let's go to the park – make the most of it while we still can.

Maru   I'm sorry, Fin, but I can't be late home tonight – it's Friday, you know what my parents are like.

Fin   Just for a bit – it'll do your breathing good.

Maru   Okay, but only for ten minutes, then I'm gone.

Maru *and* **Fin** *are once more absorbed into the city on the move until it clears again and we find them in the park beneath a large tree.*

Maru *takes in a lungful of air and then exhales, with no sign of any coughing or wheezing.*

Maru   It's so beautiful here.

Fin   Told you it'd help with your breathing.

Maru   It never fails.

Fin   How can they even think about destroying this place?

Maru   Chopping down all these trees and flattening the earth.

Fin   All the times we played hide and seek in those bushes.

Maru   I've still got scars on my knees from all the scratches I got!

Fin   It was worth it though wasn't it?

Maru   Course it was!

Beat.

You know, they didn't even ask for our opinion.

Maru *'s coughing starts to return.*

Fin They don't need to – we can't vote!

Maru But it's our future they're shaping. And our children's future! Imagine that swing – gone!

Fin All the times we've swung on it!

Maru And all the children still to come, who'll have nowhere to play!

Fin I think my dad's going to vote for him.

Maru No, he can't. You've got to stop him.

Fin He won't listen to me. He likes Bobby. Everybody likes Bobby.

Maru Why?

Fin Because Bobby's going to make everything grow again. Least that's what he says.

Maru *starts coughing sharply now.*

Fin Where's your inhaler?

Maru (*looking through her bag*)   I can't find it – I must've left it at home.

Fin (*rubbing* **Maru** *'s back*)   Breathe, Maru, breathe! You have to carry your inhaler.

Maru I just want to be able to breathe without it!

Fin Relax. In and out. (*Pause.*) Guess what?

Maru What?

Fin My mum bought another 'bag for life' yesterday!

Maru *laughs, triggering the cough again.*

Maru Don't make me laugh! How many lives is that now?

Fin Well, this is probably her twentieth – it was the blue swirling patterns, too pretty to resist!

Maru At least you know what to get her for her birthday!

Fin Talking of birthdays . . . how does it feel to be almost a teenager?

Maru Not much different, to be honest.

Fin But it is different. You'll be able to do more stuff, and people will start treating you differently, listening to you.

Maru Not my parents – and if they don't listen, why should anyone else?

Fin Well, I wish it were me!

Maru Five months will pass quickly.

Beat.

Fin   We should mark it!

Maru   Mark it?

Fin   I mean, it's important, isn't it?

Maru   I suppose so.

Fin   Have you got some paper?

Maru   I've got my detention slip!

Maru *tears off a blank section from the bottom, whilst* **Fin** *gets the pens they were given by the* **Campaigners** *out of her pocket.*

Fin   Might as well use the pens!

Maru *tears the blank paper in two, gives one half to* **Fin** *and stuffs the detention slip back into her schoolbag.*

Fin   Write down your biggest wish.

Maru   Ok!

Fin   And I'll write what I wish for you.

They turn away from each other and write.

Fin (*turning back*)   I'm done.

Maru (*turning back*)   Me too!

Fin   You go first.

Maru   I wish for the freedom to breathe!

Fin   And I wish for your voice to be heard.

Maru   What, by my teacher, you mean?

Fin   Yeah, but not just her, others too, like the people who want to build on our park.

Maru   Yeah. Thank you!

They hug.

Fin   Now, we bury them.

Fin *digs with her fingers.*

Maru   Dig deep, so no one finds them.

Maru *places the papers in the hole and* **Fin** *covers them over.* **Fin** *looks at her dirty hands, laughing. They prompt another idea.*

Fin   Have you got your water bottle?

Maru *gets out her water bottle.*

Fin Pour some here.

Fin *indicates the area that has been dug up, mixes the soil and water into a paste and then turns to* **Maru** *with muddy fingers.*

Sit still.

Fin *starts to hum as she uses the mud to carefully paint marks onto* **Maru**'s *face. At the end,* **Fin** *takes* **Maru**'s *hand and clasps it, holding tight . . .*

Fin I hereby mark you with the soil from beneath our tree . . . that you may be rooted in the earth, whilst reaching out with your branches to breathe . . .

The ritual is interrupted by a text arriving on **Maru**'s *phone.*

Maru It's my mum – she's nearly home! (*Heading off.*) I'd better go. (*Turning back.*) Thanks, Fin! (*Exits.*)

Fin See you tomorrow!

The city once more crosses, driving **Fin** *from the park. When it clears, we are in the family living room.*

Into:

Scene Two: Home (Before)

Parent One *enters with* **Georgie**, *who is full of energy.* **Parent One** *has shopping bags, and* **Georgie** *has school bags.* **Georgie** *drops coat, hat and bag as she runs around the table several times. They're in an open-plan living room. During the following,* **Parent One** *puts down bags, looks through mail, puts a parcel to one side and takes off coat.*

Georgie Maru! We're home! (*To* **Parent One**.) Can I play Nintendo?

Parent One Shoes off!

Georgie (*taking off shoes*). Now can I?

Parent One You know the drill! Ten . . . nine . . . eight –

Georgie *is running round, hanging up coat, emptying bag, wiping down table, tidying chairs round table.*

Parent One Seven . . . Maru? Sandwich box!

Georgie *arrives with homework diary.* **Parent One** *looks through.*

Parent One You've got a lot of homework!

Georgie I can do it tomorrow!

Parent One (*giving back the book*) I want to see it when you're done . . . six . . . sandwich box? . . . five . . . you're running out of time . . . four –

Georgie I'm getting it!

Parent One I'm putting the dish washer on! . . . three . . . two . . . one.

Georgie   Here. (*Handing over the sandwich box.*) Nintendo now?

Parent One   Go on! Alexa – set the timer for ten minutes!

Parent One *checks the sandwich box.*

Why didn't you eat your sandwiches? I even cut the crusts cut off!

Georgie   I wasn't hungry.

Parent One   You've managed to eat the chocolate bar. And some crisps! I didn't even give you crisps.

Georgie   Susan had two bags, so she gave me one.

Parent One   And you want to end up looking like Susan?

Georgie   She's really nice!

Parent One   Susan is a girl who eats nothing but crisps. I don't want you turning out like her. Eat your sandwiches!

Georgie   Yes, Mum.

Parent One   Good. You've got eight minutes left.

Georgie *rushes to the floor and starts playing a computer game.*

Parent One (*tidying kitchen*)   Maru! I hope you're doing your homework?! I want to see some good grades!

Luca *arrives home, throwing coat on the floor.*

Parent One   Coat. Hang it up!

Luca *picks coat up, drops on chair.*

Parent One   Hang it up!

Luca *hangs up coat, then heads for cupboard in search of food.*

Parent One   What are you doing?

Luca   Getting something to eat!

Parent One   Another snack.

Luca   I'm hungry!

Parent One   It's Friday – you know food will be here in twenty minutes.

Luca   Okay! (*But still sneaks a snack as soon as* **Parent One** *isn't looking.*)

Parent One (*waving parcel*)   Oh, and another package came for you!

Luca   Thanks!

Parent One   Thought you were saving for driving lessons?

Luca   I still need clothes to wear!

Parent One   You don't wear half the clothes you've got hanging in your wardrobe.

Luca   S'alright, none of the stuff I buy is expensive. (*Goes to play with* **Georgie** *on the Nintendo.*)

Georgie   Do you want to play Mario Cart?

Luca   200cc . . .

Georgie   200cc? No, that's too fast!

Luca   . . . and Rainbow Road . . .

Georgie   Rainbow Road?!

Luca   3-2-1 go!

*They settle into playing, making a lot of noise. Shouts of 'Get out of the way, Luigi!',
etc.* **Maru** *tries to creep in, signalling to* **Georgie** *and* **Luca** *not to let on to* **Parent
One** *that she's only just got home.* **Georgie** *stops playing, trying to understand*
Maru*'s gestures, so* **Luca** *stops, too. The silence draws attention to the situation and*
Parent One *turns round and sees* **Maru**. **Georgie** *and* **Luca** *become avid spectators.*

Parent One   Where have you been?

Maru   I lost track of time.

Parent One   I thought you were up in your room! It's nearly six!

Maru   I got distracted –

Parent One   Did you walk home again?

Maru   Yes.

Parent One   Maru, how many times?! You're not well –

Maru   Mum, I'm fine.

Parent One   I pay money for you to get a bus pass so you can stay away from the
fumes from all those cars . . .

Maru   I walked through the park.

Parent One   Did you have your inhaler?

Maru   Yes! And Fin looked after me.

Parent One   So you had an asthma attack!

Maru   Yes! No . . . yes.

Parent One (*hugging* **Maru**)   Are you ok? (*Holding* **Maru***'s face.*) Darling, your
health is not to be messed with. And what's that on your face?

Maru   It's just a bit of mud.

Parent One   Oh, please don't tell me you walked past Janet's house with that mud
on your face!

Maru   I walked past quickly . . .

Parent One   Oh Lord! She'll be walking around with those dogs of hers, telling everyone how my daughter had mud on her face.

Maru   Mum – calm down!

Parent One   Give me your sandwich box!

Maru *digs in the bag for her sandwich box and the detention slip falls out.*

Parent One (*unfolding it*)   What's this?

Georgie   You got a detention!

Luca   Maru!

Parent One (*reading slip*)   What happened?

Maru   It wasn't my fault! It was these kids . . .

Parent One   And have they got detention slips as well?

Maru   No.

Parent One   Just you?

Maru   Yes.

Parent One   Maru – keep your head down and get on with your work! We can't afford to be drawing attention to ourselves.

Parent Two *arrives home with bags full of takeaway food and fizzy drinks in single-use packaging.*

Parent Two   Hello, family! Who's ready for takeaway?!

Georgie   Dad! (*Runs to hug* **Parent Two**, **Parent Two** *hugs* **Georgie** *with bags in hand.*)

Parent Two   Traffic was terrible – hope the food's still hot. (*Kisses* **Parent One**.)

Luca   I'm starving!

Parent Two   As usual!

Everyone stands around the table expectantly.

Georgie – meat feast pizza for you – your favourite. Luca – there's your kebab.

Luca   Georgie, get some forks.

Parent Two   I brought plenty of the little plastic ones!

Maru *quietly goes to get a metal fork.*

Parent Two (*to* **Parent One**)   For you, Singapore fried rice with extra beef, some pork balls and sweet and sour sauce. And a side of ribs just in case. That's my Singapore fried rice and some chicken wings. Maru, you've been a bit picky recently, so I bought you a mega super box with a bit of everything. And drinks for the kids. (*Takes out cans of fizzy drink.*)

Parent One   Luca – do you want to say grace?

Luca   Good food, good meat, good God, let's eat!

The family unpack and dive in hungrily. The groaning sound returns, but only **Maru** *notices – and still just as a sense of unease, rather than as a sound that can be heard.*

Luca   Pass the remote.

Georgie   Put on the movie channel.

Parent Two   Hang on. I want to hear the news first.

During the news report, **Parent Two** *stares at the TV as if what is being reported is normal, while* **Parent One** *surfs the internet on a mobile.*

Reporter   . . . Quake-like cracks have appeared in several rural villages in the north of Zimbabwe. Geological and climate specialists from across the world are gathering in the capital Harare to discuss their response, in the wake of similar cracks in Bangladesh, Greenland and Papua New Guinea. The conditions in Zimbabwe are particularly –

Luca (*looking for person with the remote*)   It's boring!

Parent Two (*turning the TV over*)   Why do they always have to share bad news?

There is canned laughter coming from the TV from the new programme, a comedy.

Parent One   Oh, look at that little dog on a bicycle!

They all laugh, except **Maru**, *who is playing with her food.*

Maru   Maybe we should do something to help?

Parent Two *turns the TV off.*

Parent One   Unfortunately in countries like that, these things happen. There's nothing we can do about it.

Parent Two   You're just picking.

Maru   I don't really like the food.

Luca   It's because Maru's turned vegan.

Parent Two *laughs. No one else does. There is silence.*

Parent Two   You're not joking?

Parent One   What do you mean you turned vegan?

Luca *and* **Georgie** *sneak off to watch TV.*

Maru   I just decided not to eat meat anymore.

Parent Two   I work hard to earn the money to provide you with good food and now you're vegan, you're not going to eat it all of a sudden? Maru, there are kids in this very city who barely have enough to eat.

Georgie   Can we talk about this later?

Parent Two   You can be vegan in your own time, not in this house.

Georgie   I want to watch the film!

Parent One   You know she got a detention today?

Parent Two   Detention?

Parent One   Maru – explain to your father.

Maru   These kids were playing around with all this paper and they put it in the wrong basket – so I calmly tried to encourage them to consider using less paper and to recycle what they had used . . . and the teacher –

Parent Two   So now you're a vegan – and an activist as well?

Parent One   Next she'll be joining Extinction Rebellion and lying down in the street.

Luca   Detention Rebellion more like!

Parent Two   I learned the hard way, Maru. Standing up for yourself gets you nowhere in life. Tomorrow they'll still be throwing rubbish in the wrong bin and what are you going to do? Get yourself excluded?

Maru *clearly starts to get agitated and starts breathing heavily.*

Maru (*getting up abruptly*)   I've got homework to do . . .

Parent One   Good, do your homework, but listen to your father – what he's saying is true.

Maaru   I will.

Parent One (*calling after* **Maru**)   And take your inhaler – I can hear you wheezing from here.

Maru   Ok.

Maru *exits. The family transform the furniture of the living room into the furniture of* **Maru***'s bedroom.*

Into:

Scene Three: Bedroom

Maru *goes to the bed, takes out her inhaler and looks at it – then puts it to one side and, instead, takes out a book from under the pillow. She sits on the floor and starts to read. As she reads, the story calms her, and the world of the story starts to come to life in the bedroom.*

Maru   Once there was a girl who wanted to plant a garden. (**Maru** *breathes deeply.*)

She was born in a village, where life was precious, and in a land that was plentiful, but where seasons could be fierce. (**Maru** *takes another breath, becoming calmer.*)

Her Mother showed her how to plant vegetables – rich roots, succulent fruits and fresh leaves.

And in the centre of the garden, she planted a beautiful tree.
She watered and tended the tree every day, singing as she worked.
And sometimes, the tree sang back to her:

Tree   If ever it may seem
Like there may be no tomorrow,
Plant one small seed
It may grow to feed a village.

Maru   And as she grew, so did the tree.
And when it was grown, Mother and Daughter would sit under its wondrous branches, grateful for the shade it provided from the hot summer sun and the shelter from the rain.

Over the course of time, the girl's village suffered a drought, one that devastated much of her country and the hearts of her people.

There was barely enough water to drink and slowly the girl's garden withered away.

Before long, they were down to their last calabash of water.

Mother   Drink, Daughter, for you have all your life to live and mine is nearly at its end.

Maru   So the Daughter drank, and they sat under the tree. And in the morning, the Mother did not wake.

They buried her body under the tree, and the girl watered the ground with her tears.

The following year, the rains returned and with the rain the tree grew to become a mighty and wondrous memorial to the Mother. For the first time, it bore fruit and the whole village came to gather its juicy flesh.

The girl was happy for the villagers to eat their fill, provided they watered the tree after each visit:

Maru   'Eat, but please – remember my mother who cares for the roots.'

To begin with, the people did as she asked.

But as time wore on, they began to neglect this simple request.

Villager One   The roots of that tree are too thirsty.

Villager Two   I have just enough water for myself.

Villager Three   I didn't even know her mother!

Maru   Before long, people were coming from far and wide to take fruit from the tree. Some even set up stalls to sell what they had picked, trampling over its drying roots without a thought as to how it would survive.

The earth became dry as a desert and as hard as a rock.

The fruit became scarcer and scarcer.

Until one day, the earth was so dry that it split in two and a giant crack tore through the centre of the village. (*Inhalation.*)

Luca (*from outside the room*).   Maru!

Luca *knocks and the Village scene evaporates.* **Luca** *enters.*

Luca   You've got to clear the draining board!

Maru   But I hoovered the whole living room yesterday!

Luca   Still your turn to do the draining board!

Maru   Leave me alone!

Luca (*shrugging*)   You'll have Mum to answer to if you don't.

Luca *leaves.* **Maru** *is pensive. She hides the book again.*

The family reverse the previous transition – back from bedroom into living room.

Into:

Scene Four: Transitions

Bobby Brunt *is having tea with* **Maru**'s **Parents** *in their living room.*

Brunt   . . . and I've always believed that the working man must come first! Jobs for British workers, investment in car manufacturing – make this city great again!

Parent Two   That's what I've always said!

Brunt   Of course you have, and you're 100 per cent right! Which is why I'm *personally* visiting factory workers like yourself to give you some assurances – like I always say, 'There's no front with Brunt!'

Parent One   Cup of tea, Mr Brunt?

Brunt   Nothing like a good cup of English tea.

Parent One *goes to pour it.*

Brunt   No, please, allow me – it's what this campaign is all about – me serving you!

Parent One   Ooh, thank you! Some cake?

Brunt *pats his waistline and shakes his head as if to say, 'I couldn't possibly!'*

Parent Two   She's hands down the best baker on this street!

Brunt   You've twisted my arm! (*Taking a bite.*) Oh now, that's amazing – what a woman!

Parent One *is coy but proud.* **Brunt** *stands to leave.*

Brunt   Right, I'm afraid I have to drag myself away – got lots of other hard-working people to see this afternoon. But it's been an absolute pleasure to meet you both.

Parent Two   You too – you're a breath of fresh air, Mr Brunt!

Brunt   Please – call me Bobby – we're friends now!

Parent Two   Thanks, Bobby!

They shake hands enthusiastically. As **Brunt** *prepares to leave,* **Maru** *and* **Fin** *come through the door and are stunned to see him.*

Maru   What's he doing here?

Parent One   Darling, this is –

Maru   Bobby Brunt.

Parent Two   Yes – and he's going to be the new mayor!

Brunt   So I can count on your votes then?

Parents   Yes!

Brunt *shakes their hands again, and puts his hand out for* **Fin**.

Brunt   Hello! (**Brunt** *forms a fist bump which* **Fin** *reluctantly reciprocates.*)

Brunt *then tries the same with* **Maru**, *who ignores the fist altogether.*

Parent One   Maru!

Maru   He's going to destroy our park!

Fin   Digging it all up to make houses!

Brunt   Workers need places to live. Plenty of parks on the outskirts. We need to make compromises to move forward.

Parent Two   More jobs coming – good news for your Dad, Fin, down at the car plant!

Maru   So more cars polluting the city!

Brunt   Ah, but these are electric cars!

Maru   Electric cars still need energy to power them!

Brunt   I care as much about the environment as you do – but I've been to China and the pollution is terrible. There's really no point in doing anything about it here until they do . . . in 2050, say . . .

Maru   By that time half the country could be under water!

Parent One (*embarrassed and trying to lighten the mood*)   Turning thirteen today, lots of opinions!

Brunt   Ahhh! Happy birthday – I think this calls for a 'Bobby Brunt for Mayor' lollipop.

Maru (*disgusted*)   It's got your face on it!

Brunt   So it has! Kids . . . are our future! Best be off! (*As he disappears.*) Lobby for Bobby!

Brunt *leaves.* **Parent One** *looks disappointed at* **Maru** *and is about to say something but* **Parent Two** *stops her.*

Parent One   Time to celebrate someone's birthday! (*Opens arms to embrace.*) I can't believe my little girl's thirteen!

Parent Two   Georgie, Luca! Maru's home!

Georgie *runs in.*

Parent One   A new chapter, fresh responsibilities!

Luca *runs in.*

Maru   Thanks, Mum!

Georgie   You've got presents to open!

Luca   Happy birthday, Maru!

Parent One   And we've got a special surprise for you upstairs.

Maru   Seriously?!

Parent One   Close your eyes!

Parent One *covers* **Maru***'s eyes, whilst the family once more set up the bedroom in front of her. This time, however, the bedroom is different. It is now a modern room, with new matching units and a fresh, cool colour scheme.*

Parent One   You can open them now!

Parents   Surprise! / Ta dah!

Parent One *takes her hands from* **Maru***'s eyes.* **Maru** *is stunned.*

Maru   Oh my God!

Parent One   You love it, right?

Fin   This is sick!

Fin *starts moving around the room, checking all the new features.* **Maru** *is adjusting to the new space.*

Parent One   Everything matches now – curtains, bed covers, new wardrobe, bigger desk for studying, bigger bookshelf for your books –

Maru   I liked my old bookshelf.

Parent Two   Yes, but this is all from that massive new Swedish shop –

Parent One   Cost a small fortune –

Parent Two   Been doing overtime for weeks –

Parent One   But you deserve it! Happy birthday!

Luca   I never got this for my thirteenth!

Parent Two   Well, you had a big party!

Fin   I wish my room was like this!

Maru   It's . . . wonderful!

Parent One   You've got a mirror now so you can do your hair and things! And there are lights in it!

Maru   I can see that.

Parent Two   Much more grown-up!

Maru   I love it!

Parent One   We knew you would!

Maru (*looking for her book in the usual place under her pillow*)   My other things. What did you do with them?

Parent One   You'll be pleased to know we listened to your advice –

Parent Two   Reuse, recycle, reduce –

Parent One   Nothing wasted!

Maru   But my book – I had a book, with a red cover?

Fin   Your storybook?

Maru   Yes!

Parent Two   Didn't think you'd want it anymore now you're growing up . . .

Parent One   Got to focus on your studies . . .

Parent Two   We gave it to a charity shop. Some other child will get to enjoy it, just like you did.

Maru   Right. (**Maru**'s *breathing is starting to get difficult again.*)

Parent Two   Can see you're overwhelmed. We'll leave you two to chat!

Parent One   Don't be too long – there's cake downstairs!

Parents *leave and* **Maru** *collapses in a heap. She is devastated, panicking and struggling to breath.*

Fin   What's wrong?

Maru   My whole room has gone!

Fin   But this is so cool!

Maru   But I didn't *need* any of it!

Fin   They wanted your thirteenth to feel special.

Maru   I get that, but I can't believe they got rid of my book!

Fin   They probably just thought you'd grown out of it.

Maru   Who's side are you on, Fin?

Maru's *crying and coughing gets worse.*

Fin   I didn't realise it was that important to you!

Maru   Not that important?!

Maru *produces a massive barking cough, as a* **Crack** *opens up in the new bookcase.*

Fin   What the . . .?

Both **Maru** *and* **Fin**'s *eyes watch as the* **Crack** *splits the bookcase in two. They are shocked and frightened.* **Fin** *looks at* **Maru** *and is spooked. She starts to back out of the room.*

Fin   I – I need to go! I'll see you later!

Fin *leaves.* **Maru** *is curious about the* **Crack** *and approaches the bookcase. She runs her finger along the* **Crack** *as if trying to understand. The* **Crack** *seems to groan softly.*

Parent One (*shouting*)   Maru! Time for birthday cake!

Maru *reluctantly leaves her room and goes to meet the rest of the family.*

Parent Two *is holding a birthday cake.* **Parent One** *is excited.*

All (*singing*)

>   Happy birthday to you! Happy birthday to you!
>   Happy birthday, dear Maru! Happy birthday to you!

Parent One   Blow your candles out! Make a wish! Right, plates everyone!

Parent One *starts cutting and serving the cake.* **Maru** *is distracted by what just happened upstairs.*

Parent Two   Fin left in a hurry.

Maru   Oh, her Mum called.

Parent One *serves* **Maru** *a piece of cake.*

Maru   What kind of cake is it?

Parent Two   We remembered that you're vegan –

Parent One (*serving* **Luca** *a piece of cake*)   So no eggs!

Georgie (*disgusted*)   It's a vegan cake?

Maru   Great. And what did you use to replace the butter?

Parent One   Replace the butter? You can't make a cake without butter!

Maru   But butter isn't –

Georgie   So it isn't vegan! (*Digging in.*)

Parent One   I've messed it up haven't I?

Maru   No, no, I'm sure it's lovely!

Parent Two   Butter isn't vegan?

Maru   Don't worry!

Everyone goes to take a bit of their cake, and there's a sudden 'crack' from upstairs, from the direction of **Maru***'s bedroom. Everyone pauses and looks up, lowering their cake.*

Maru (*to self*)   Not again.

Parent Two   Wait here, I'll be back in a second.

Parent Two *departs to investigate.*

Parent One (*looking at* **Maru**)   What do you mean, 'again'?

Into:

Scene Four: Papering over the Cracks

Parent Two *enters* **Maru***'s room with a bucket of wallpaper paste, some brushes and a roll of wallpaper.*

Parent Two   This is a right mess, Maru. (*Shakes head.*) What happened?

Maru   I'm sorry. I don't know . . .

Parent Two (*indicating the newly decorated room*)   Look at the state of it! You've barely had the stuff for five minutes! Do you know what this cost us?

Parent Two *starts to paste the back of the wallpaper.*

Maru   It wasn't me.

Parent Two *sighs in response.*

Parent Two   Cracks don't just appear for no reason, Maru.

They continue to work at the pasting of the paper.

Honestly, the stuff you kids take for granted. You think I had this kind of luxury when I was your age?

Maru   I'll fix it. (*Pause.*) If it helps I could get the old bookshelf back from the charity shop you donated it to.

Parent Two   Right . . . (*Continues working.*)

Maru (*continues talking awkwardly*)   Fin and I could go and get it if you tell me where it is. We could get Georgie and Luca to help us –

Parent Two   And why would I pay good money for the old stuff I've just given away?

Maru   I liked it. And you wouldn't need to, I've got money saved up.

Parent Two   From your pocket money, right? The money that your mum and I work hard to give you?

Parent Two *starts to hang the wallpaper.*

Maru   Maybe I could just get my book back then?

Parent Two   What book?

Maru   The storybook you and mum gave me, it was on the bookshelf. Do you know which charity shop –

Parent Two   You want me to traipse halfway across town for a children's book? When I've got this mess to fix?

Maru   But it's . . . sentimental.

Parent Two   Sentimental! You're far too young to understand what that word means!

Maru   It's like the watch Granny gave you.

Parent Two (*looking at the watch on their wrist*)   Granny's watch is completely different. This is actually worth something.

Maru   But I need it. It's important.

Parent Two   No, Maru, it's not!

There is the sound of groaning and creaking. The papered **Crack** *rips open.*

Parent Two   No, no, no, no, no! Maru, what have you done?

Maru   I didn't touch anything!

Parent Two   Well, it's starting to look wilful to me. What's wrong with you? Any normal teenager would love to have a bedroom like this.

A loud 'crack' is heard from downstairs.

Georgie (*from off*)   Dad, you'd better come quick, there's a crack in the living room now as well!

Parent Two *looks at* **Maru**, *shakes their head despairingly and then leaves.* **Maru** *is mesmerised by the* **Crack**.

Maru   It's just like the story!

Suddenly a sound like an inhalation comes from the **Crack**. **Maru** *looks into it.*

Maru   Hello?

The **Crack** *answers back with a breathy exhalation.*

Into:

The bedroom clears and we see **Maru** *looking for her book in a charity shop. She can't find it.*

Into:

Scene Six: Home (After)

Parent One *enters with* **Georgie**. **Parent One** *has shopping bags, and* **Georgie** *is keen to play a game. There is now a huge* **Crack** *down the centre of the living room. The family have to walk carefully around it, wary of making it worse. Each are mindful of it in their own way –* **Georgie** *afraid,* **Parent One** *anxious,* **Luca** *resentful/curious,* **Parent Two** *undermined. This is important in colouring the scene differently from Scene Two.*

Georgie *circles the crack and goes straight to sit at the Nintendo.*

Parent One   Have you done your homework?

Georgie (*evasively*)   Yes!

Parent One   What about your chores? (*Silence from* **Georgie**.) Ten . . . nine . . . eight –

Georgie *is running round, hanging up coat, emptying bag, but is having to be careful around the* **Crack**.

Parent One   Seven . . . Maru? Downstairs! . . . Six . . . Lord! That child! Five . . . four –

Georgie   Mum, I can't do it! (*Looking at the* **Crack**.) It's too hard now!

Parent One   I know, baby. But it's just the way things are at the moment. Best not to make a fuss. We'll work round it.

Luca *enters and is about to dump her coat.*

Parent One   Coat! And before you ask, there's nothing to eat. I've not been to the shops. Couldn't face . . . all those people outside our house, pointing and staring . . . . making up excuses for walking past here . . . to judge. . . . Your dad will be back soon, so you'll have to wait.

Luca   Aw, Mum –

Parent One   Look, there's some stale cake on the kitchen counter if you're that desperate! Now leave me be! And you (*to* **Georgie**) – sandwich box?

Georgie *hands over a full sandwich box then goes and sits in front of the TV to play either game on one side of the* **Crack**.

Parent One   Er . . . what's this?

Georgie   I had a few packets of crisps . . . I was too full to eat it. Susan gave me –

Parent One   I don't want to hear it!

Luca   Anything arrive for me?

Parent One   On the table. You'd better still have enough savings for those driving lessons –

Luca   Okay, Mum!

Luca *backs away and goes to sit with* **Georgie**, *but on the other side of the* **Crack**.

Luca   Ok, Rainbow Road, 200CC?

Georgie   Again?

Luca   Ready?

They begin to play the game. There's a good-natured competitive rivalry between the siblings and **Georgie** *is glad of the distraction from the* **Crack**.

Georgie   Why do you always do this?

Luca   What? Win?

Parent One (*calling off*)   Maru!

Parent One *takes out their laptop and starts reading.* **Luca** *opens the package and examines the new purchase, an item of clothing, fast fashion – she can take it or leave it. She discards it, indifferent to her wastefulness, and starts playing the game with* **Georgie**.

Maru *creeps in.* **Georgie** *and* **Luca** *stop playing.* **Maru** *gestures to them to keep making a noise, but they don't understand.* **Parent One** *notices.*

Parent One   Maru! Late again!

Maru   I'm sorry –

Parent One   Were you ill? Sit down! How's your breathing?

Maru   Honestly, I'm OK!

Parent One *sighs and rummages for* **Maru**'s *sandwich box.*

Maru   Mum – stop! – I can do it . . .

Parent One (*taking kitchen implement out of bag*)   What is this? (*Outrage.*) British Heart Foundation?

Maru   I thought it might be useful – Dad dropped ours down the crack.

Parent One   Stop buying things at charity shops! People will think we can't buy new!

Maru   I just want to find my book –

Parent One   Did you walk?

Maru Yes I walked and I'm fine!

Parent One What is wrong with you? You know how I worry and yet you seem determined to drive me crazy!

Parent Two *arrives home with takeaway boxes and soft drinks in plastic bottles.*

Parent Two Hello, family! Help me please!

Georgie Dad!

Georgie *runs to hug* **Parent Two**, *jumping over* **Crack**. **Parents** *share a perfunctory kiss.* **Parent Two** *hands out the meals – first to* **Georgie**, *who runs to sit by the Nintendo.* **Luca** *takes her own food and joins* **Georgie**.

Parent One Maru was late again. Walking through smog to find some rubbish in a charity shop.

Maru It's not rubbish!

Parent Two It's been a long day. I can't cope with this at the minute.

Parent One Did you get my sweet and sour pork and special fried rice?

Parent Two As always. And for us (*referring to* **Maru**) – I thought I'd try being vegan too – I got us fish and chips.

Maru Oh . . .

Maru *takes the food in silence.* **Maru** *and* **Parent One** *sit at the table to eat their supper.* **Parent Two** *leaves their supper on the table, gets some plaster out of a bag and starts inspecting the* **Crack** *under the table.*

Parent One Darling . . .?

Parent Two *looks up, bumping their head on the table.*

Parent One Please come and eat your food.

Parent Two I will. But I need to do something about this first.

Parent Two *starts filling the* **Crack** *with plaster, patching it up.*

Parent One Ignore it for now. It'll be fine.

Parent Two (*from under the table*). It won't fix itself.

Parent One But your dinner is –

Parent Two *stands up and almost topples the table. The rest of the family steady it.*

Parent Two You scrimp and save for a new house, you believe all the stuff those developers say, and then this! Right out of the blue!

Parent One Well, banging around and shouting isn't going to help. I don't want the neighbours thinking we've got problems!

Parent Two   We have got problems! And they don't come much bigger than having a massive crack right through the middle of your living-room floor!

Parent One   Tone it down! Kids, eat your food! Maru, you've haven't even touched yours!

Maru   It's fish.

Parent Two   I can't keep up with you – I thought you were a vegan?

Parent One   No more meat – that's right isn't it?

Maru   No animal products at all. I can maybe eat the chips.

Parent Two   Oh, that's very kind of you – haven't completely wasted my hard-earned cash!

Maru   Dad! I'm standing up for what I believe in – don't you want me to have values?

Parent One   Of course we do, but this is not the way! You living on veg isn't going to change the world. Best you can do is keep your head down. Believe me, there are worse things than eating meat.

Luca *throws a napkin down the* **Crack**. **Maru** *starts wheezing.*

Parent One   You okay, love?

Maru *coughs.* **Luca** *notices, looks puzzled and throws another piece of rubbish down the* **Crack***, watching* **Maru** *carefully.* **Maru** *coughs more.*

Parent One   Where's your inhaler?

Maru *points at her coat.* **Parent Two** *runs and grabs the inhaler from the pocket.* *Both* **Parents** *help* **Maru***, and her breathing calms.*

Luca *takes the packaging from her parcel and throws it down the* **Crack***.* **Maru** *starts wheezing again.* **Luca** *knows there is some connection.* **Maru** *and* **Luca** *lock eyes.*

Maru (*getting up*)   I just need to find my book.

Parent One   Nonsense, you can't breathe, you need to lie down and prop yourself up.

Maru   Please, I need it!

Parent One   How's a kids' book going to make you better?

Maru (*searching for an explanation*)   I can't explain it. Once I've found it, I'll show you.

Maru *grabs her coat and heads for the door.*

Parent One   Maru, come back this minute. (**Maru** *leaves.*) You've left your inhaler!

Into:

Scene Seven: The Crack Spreads to the City

Maru *continues her search for the storybook in another charity shop, but still does not find it. She is becoming desperate.*

The people of the city continue in their wasteful ways, oblivious to their role in creating the **Crack.**

Into:

A bake sale on the street outside **Maru**'*s family home. Two* **Neighbours** *stand next to a small cake stand. They are gossiping about the recent appearance of the* **Crack,** *which is now visible from the outside of the house.*

Neighbour One (*admiring their handiwork*)   Your red velvet looks delicious!

Neighbour Two   Not as good as your Black Forest gateau!

Neighbour One   It'd be absolutely perfect, if it wasn't for one thing . . . (*They look at the* **Crack.**)

Neighbour One *and* **Two**   . . . that crack!

Neighbour One   I mean, who wants to come to a cake sale on Crack Street?!

Neighbour Two   And what if it spreads down the street? I don't want my house devalued because they can't afford to do repairs!

Neighbour Two   I know! I mean, I'm not a nosey person, but I was doing my morning jog and I couldn't help but see into the house . . . and the crack . . . it's so big! . . . (*Looks over her shoulder.*) And they've got yellow wallpaper!

They both laugh.

And you should see the carpet!

Neighbour One   You never know what's behind closed doors. Oh, did I tell you? My Sophie wanted to donate some money to that village in the Philippines – the one with the tornado . . .

Neighbour Two   Bless her little heart!

Neighbour One   Well, she also wants the new iPhone . . .

Neighbour Two   . . . and you know what they cost!

Neighbour One   I said, 'Sophie, it's either iPhone or tornado.'

Neighbour Two   I mean you can't do everything can you?

Brunt *and* **Aide** *arrive on the street.* **Brunt** *makes a beeline for the group.*

Brunt   Good afternoon, lovely people!

The group spots **Brunt** *and immediately stop talking. It's as if they're in the presence of a celebrity. They smile and laugh, ready to hang off* **Brunt**'*s every word.*

Brunt (*shaking hands with each of them*)   Bobby Brunt . . . Hi, Bobby Brunt . . . Nice to meet you – Bobby Brunt. Nice cakes! They smell divine!

Neighbour One   Please, have a cookie.

Neighbour One *offers* **Brunt** *a cookie.* **Bobby** *takes a bite from it.*

Brunt   Mmm, delicious. (*Pocketing the cookie and brushing the crumbs from his hands.*) Now, can I tell you lovely ladies about my plans to . . .

A **New Parent** *carrying a baby appears.*

Brunt   One second . . . (*Rushing over to the* **New Parent** *and baby.*) What a lovely baby! Do you mind if I hold it?

The **New Parent** *is hesitant but has no choice.* **Brunt** *takes the baby and poses next to the* **New Parent***, as the* **Aide** *hurries forward to take a photograph. As soon as they have the picture* **Brunt** *dumps the baby back in the arms of the parent, and hurries off to their next official engagement.*

Into:

Fin *and* **Parent** *trying on clothes in a shop.* **Fin's Parent** *holds up a jacket. It's a very trendy piece of clothing, something that is unlikely to be worn for more than a few weeks.*

Parent   I do quite like it . . .

Fin   You bought a coat last week.

Parent   I'm gonna try it on. (*Puts on the jacket, which is clearly too small.*) What do you think?

Fin   Er, maybe you should get a slightly bigger size?

Parent   They don't have a bigger one, but I really like it . . . I reckon I can lose the weight! (*Looks at the tag.*) It's so cheap.

Fin   But do you *need* it?

Parent   I'm going to get it!

Fin's Parent *goes off to the cash desk.* **Fin** *goes to follow, then makes a quick decision to slip off to look for* **Maru***.*

Into:

Parent *and* **Child** *sitting in the front seats of a car. They are stuck in traffic.*

Child (*impatiently*)   Why did we have to drive?

Parent   I'm not walking around in this cold weather.

Child   I know, but it's like five minutes away, and now we're stuck in all this traffic.

Parent (*beeping the horn at the car in front*)   Move, you wanker!

Driver (*winding down their car window*)   Do you mind?!

Child   Wait, is that Tilly's dad?

Parent (*embarrassed*)   I'll speak to him in church on Sunday!

Parent *waves at the* **Driver**, *to hopefully placate them. Traffic starts to move.*

Into:

Maru *continues the search for the storybook in another charity shop – but still doesn't find it.*

Into:

There is the sound of a huge 'crack'. Bigger than any that have gone before.

The whole stage splits in two as the **Crack** *spreads from the house to the city.*

Into:

Brunt *is with a bunch of* **Young Children**, *at a library, reading them a book. There is a* **Camera Person** *present recording the event.*

Brunt   . . . so she took it to the garage in the village, where Paddy fixed the engine – but what happened? That's right, the little red car got stuck in the mud again! We can't be having that can we?

Children   No!

Brunt's **Aide** *gets a call and is flustered.*

Brunt   Well, you'll be pleased to know, my young followers, that as Mayor, I will be directing our investment –

Aide   Sorry, Mr Brunt. Something is happening in the centre. It seems a massive crack has appeared – some kind of disaster!

Brunt *looks awkwardly to the* **Camera Person** *who is capturing the moment.*

Brunt   So the dwarves all lived happily ever after. The end. Got to go!

Brunt *throws the book at one of the* **Children** *to catch and struts off with the* **Aide**, *leaving the* **Children** *behind.*

Into:

Scene Eight: Exploiting the Crack

The **City Dwellers** *are going about their day-to-day lives, either ignoring the* **Crack**, *or exploiting it for their own gain.*

A **Chancer** *is trying to sell T-shirts and tours of the* **Crack**.

Chancer   Come and get your original 'CRACKING UP' T-shirt! One-time special offer, ten pounds with every ticket booked for the exclusive 'Crack' tour!

A **City Dweller** *crosses, unperturbed by the* **Crack***.*

Chancer   Not to be missed, get your tickets now!

A **City Dweller** *crosses, completely uninterested – they've got places to go . . .*

A **YouTuber** *is filming a post about the* **Crack***:*

YouTuber   What's up, guys! Welcome back to the channel. Today we're at 'the Crack'. Wow! It's really deep and dark – it feels like it could go through to the other side of the world! We're going to have a look around and chat to a few people. Remember, click 'like' and 'subscribe'!

Chancer (*to* **YouTuber**)   Can I interest you in a 'CRACKING UP' T-shirt? Only ten pounds with a ticket for the exclusive 'Crack tour'!

YouTuber   'Crack tour'? Yes, please!

A group of **Parkour Youths** *arrive to explore the possibilities of the* **Crack***. They put pay to* **Chancer***'s 'Crack' tour. They take it in turns to do daring leaps over the* **Crack***, cheering each other after each leap.* **Chancer** *joins the cheers, offers T-shirts,* **YouTuber** *films.*

A **Negative Nelly** *approaches the* **Crack** *and susses out its possibilities for an insurance claim. When the others are cheering the* **Parkour Youths***, she walks over the* **Crack** *and pretends to trip.*

Nelly   You saw that didn't you? I just damaged my ankle! Get me the council's number! I'm contacting 'Injury Specialists dot com' – I'm suing! I've had an accident and it wasn't my fault!

The **Parkour Youths** *help her up.* **Chancer** *offers her a discounted T-shirt.* **Chancer** *and* **Negative Nelly** *exit.*

A **Journalist** *enters and is practising lines in front of a* **Camera Person***. The* **Parkour Youths** *notice and try to sneak into shot.*

Maru *enters and watches the way the* **Crack** *is being treated.*

Journalist   'Environmental crisis . . . or local neglect?' Not snappy enough!

The **Camera Person** *notices the youths and indicates to the* **Journalist** *to change position so that they are no longer in shot.*

A **Drunk** *comes in and uses the* **Crack** *for a quick pee.*

Journalist   'Climate catastrophe or domestic disaster' – what do you think?

Camera Person *indicates to the* **Journalist** *that there is a problem.*

Journalist *turns to see the* **Drunk** *in shot.*

A **Pastor** *enters wearing a sign which reads 'The End Is Nigh'.*

Pastor (*to the* **Drunk**)   Change your ways before it's too late! The Devil, he is coming up through the depths of hell!

So, get your place in heaven!

Camera Person   Hey! Could you be quiet – we're trying to film!

Journalist *indicates to the* **Camera Person** *to find a different angle.*

Pastor (*to* **Maru**, *warning*)   Turn your life around! (*Exits.*)

Journalist   Whilst parallels are being drawn with the freak cracks appearing in countries across the globe, this crack seems to have originated with just one family located in the northern suburbs of the city. Authorities are requesting that people with more information should contact them immediately. Okay – that should do it. Let's go and grab a beer!

Journalist *and* **Camera Person** *exit.*

Maru *is fearful of the news she has just heard, but mesmerised by the* **Crack** *and begins to move closer.* **Fin** *appears and spots* **Maru** *leaning over the* **Crack**.

Fin   Maru! What are you doing?

Maru *turns, spots* **Fin**. *A moment of uncertainty passes between them. They embrace.*

Maru   I really missed you.

Fin   You ok? (*Beat.*)

I missed you too. I'm sorry about your bedroom, and your book. And . . . for walking out like that. I was scared.

Maru (*indicating the* **Crack**)   I did this, Fin. Everything that's happening is because of me.

Fin   It's not your fault, Maru . . . it's not.

Maru *looks doubtful.*

Fin   Ok, so let's think about it. You were in your room, you noticed your book was gone, you were coughing . . . your asthma came . . . you coughed and . . . it happened.

Maru   So I did cause it.

Fin   You didn't. It's a coincidence. These cracks have been appearing all over the world, we've all seen them.

Maru   Yes, but there weren't any here until the one in my bedroom and now they're all over the city. And everyone's saying it's my fault!

Fin   Well, they're wrong. They should be trying to do something about it instead of just going around blaming people.

Maru   Exactly. And that's why I need to find my book.

Fin   You think the answer to all of this is in your book?

Maru   If you're not going to take me seriously . . .

Fin   Sorry!

Maru   Look, I know this might sound a bit weird, but whenever I read it, I feel, I don't know, I feel like me. I can breathe again. And in one of the stories a large crack suddenly appears in the earth.

Two **Fly-Tippers** *appear carrying a large load of rubbish.*

Fly-Tipper One   It's good and wide over here, Stevie.

Fly-Tipper Two   Excuse me.

They move **Fin** *and* **Maru** *out of the way and tip the rubbish down the* **Crack**.

They exit.

Fin   Right, and then what?

Maru *starts to struggle to breathe again.*

Maru   I don't know, I haven't finished the story because my parents gave the book away!

Fin   So you think if you could read the end of the story, it might have the answer to how to get rid of all the cracks?

Maru   Exactly! But I've looked everywhere.

Fin   Let's keep trying.

Maru *is wheezing now.*

Fin (*to* **Maru**)   Are you okay?

The **Fly-Tippers** *re-enter and attempt to barge past* **Maru** *and* **Fin**.

Fin   Hey! Can't you see she's not well?

Fly-Tipper One   Can't you see I've got my hands full?

Maru *is still struggling to breathe.*

Fly-Tipper Two   Bleeding kids!

Impatient, **Fly-Tipper Two** *drags a plank out of the wheelbarrow, puts it over the* **Crack** *and indicates to* **Fly-Tipper One** *to cross over to the other side.*

Fly-Tipper Two   Here – try this!

Fly-Tipper One   Okay – 3-2-1 . . .

They empty the container into the **Crack**.

Maru's *breathing becomes suddenly worse, as if she has something lodged in her throat. The* **Fly-Tippers** *exit.*

Fin   Maru, where's your inhaler? Shall I get someone?

Maru *shakes her head, reaches into her pocket and pulls out the inhaler. After a few moments her breathing begins to ease.*

Fly-Tipper One *returns, armed with more rubbish and again tips it into the* **Crack**.

Maru   What are you doing?

Fly-Tipper One   What does it look like?

Maru   Stop it. It's not a rubbish dump.

Fly-Tipper One   Really? (*Looking down at the* **Crack**.) That's not what it looks like to me. Why don't you mind your own business?

Maru *begins to cough again.*

Fin   Don't speak to her like that.

Fly-Tipper Two *dumps their rubbish into the* **Crack**.

Fin   You should take better care of the environment!

Fly-Tipper Two   Why? What's the environment ever done for me? (*To* **Fly-Tipper One**.) Honestly, little kids that don't know when to mind their own business . . . it pisses me off, Dave!

Maru *coughs and the* **Crack** *opens up into the auditorium.*

The **Fly-Tippers** *gawp and look panicked.*

Fly-Tipper Two (*to* **Fly-Tipper One**)   You saw that right?

Fly-Tipper One (*points to* **Maru** *and* **Fin**)   What the – *you* just did that! We . . . we saw it . . . with our own eyes . . . right, Stevie? (*To* **Fly-Tipper Two**, *who takes out their phone and is taking photos.*) Stop that! Call the police or something!

Fly-Tipper Two   Wait a minute – I know you! You're the one on the news – the one from that house in the north of the city – they're calling you the 'Super Cracker'!

Fly-Tipper One *starts to phone the police.*

Maru *and* **Fin** *look shaken and quickly leave.*

Fly-Tipper Two *is glued to their screen.*

Fly-Tipper One   The line's jammed. Must be something going on. What you doing?

Fly-Tipper One   Just updating Twitter – I can't believe what I just saw!

Fly-Tipper Two   I know, mate (*taking selfie*) – weird!

Into:

Scene Nine: Chaos in the City

The **Crack** *is getting bigger, causing chaos in the city.*

A sequence of **Worried People** *enter, all observing their phones closely and tapping out messages.*

Worried One   Oh my God – crack's getting bigger – first cracks, next wars! – hashtag 'World War 3'!

Worried Two   Lord save us! My dog just fell into the crack – hashtag 'It ain't safe on these streets'!

Into:

*A **Mother** and **Child** trying to escape with all their worldly belongings packed into a few suitcases.*

Child   Mum – these are heavy – where's the car?

Mother   I could have sworn I parked it right here!

*She presses the automatic unlock button on her keys and hears a beep. It's coming from the **Crack**. They approach and look into the **Crack**. The car has fallen in.*

Child   Now what will we do?

Mother (*determinedly*)   We'll have to go with the Wilkinsons. Quick – they were leaving at three!

They run off as quickly as their luggage will allow, looking back at where the car should have been.

Into:

Worried Three   Oh, there goes the school! And there goes Greggs!

Worried Four   My city's being destroyed!

Worried Three and **Four** (*together*)   Hashtag 'Scared for my life'!

Into:

Maru and **Fin** enter as if pursued and hide behind a convenient wall. Their pursuers run past them. They are relieved as they are tired from running. **Maru** looks at her phone.

Maru   There's a photo of us!

Fin   What?

Maru   We're trending on Twitter!

Fin   Those guys with the rubbish . . . never mind, we can't think about that now . . . (*Dragging **Maru** away.*) We need to find somewhere safe.

Maru   Where? Everyone's looking for us!

Maru *starts coughing and tries her inhaler but it's empty. She carries on coughing.*

Fin (*referring to the inhaler*)   Take some more, Maru, come on, deep breaths.

Maru   No use, it's empty.

*They hear **Brunt** arriving.*

Fin   Come on, there's only one place we can go.

Fin *and* **Maru** *exit in the opposite direction.*

Into:

Brunt *enters with a* **Journalist** *and* **Camera Person** *in tow, and a small* **Crowd** *including* **Maru**'s *family.*

Brunt   Of course, we are incredibly concerned. Citizens are rightly worried about the cracks appearing across our fine city, and about the potential impact on homes and jobs. I assure you that all possible resources will be ploughed into protecting the property of honest, working local people.

And a message to this so-called 'Super Cracker' and her friend – we will not bow down to terrorists. We know who you are and we're coming to get you.

Luca   Maru isn't a terrorist! She isn't responsible for this!

Parent One (*pulling her away*)   Don't draw attention, Luca.

Brunt   We have our best people looking into this. I can assure you that –

Luca   How can you blame one individual?! There are cracks like these all over the world!

Brunt   Er . . . we need to move on. Rest assured I am leading the charge to restore our fortunes.

Another group of **Citizens** *fleeing the city cross the stage carrying suitcases and looking desperate – a contrast/parallel to the* **City Dwellers** *in the opening scene.* **Brunt** *moves away with the group.* **Luca** *wrestles free of* **Parent One** *and runs off.* **Parent One** *follows her.*

Into:

Scene Ten: Tree (After)

The park. **Maru** *and* **Fin** *enter, running, though* **Maru** *is clearly weakened.* **Fin** *supports* **Maru**, *and both look edgy, checking over their shoulders.*

A voice offstage through a loud hailer.

Brunt   Maru! Fin! We've got you surrounded. There's no escape.

The girls shrink into the tree, trying to make themselves as small as possible. **Maru** *covers her mouth with her hand to try and prevent a cough.*

Fin   He's bluffing – no one saw us come here.

Brunt (*off*)   You're not in trouble. We just want to talk to you.

Maru   I don't trust him.

Brunt (*off*)   You need help, Maru. Why don't you let us help you? (*Getting closer.*) Fin! Maru!

Fin (*whispering*)   What are we going to do?

Maru *doesn't answer.*

Fin   Maru?

Maru   I don't know! . . . I don't know how the story ends!

Fin   Then make it up!

Maru   What?

Fin   You know most of the story . . . find the ending yourself.

Maru *hesitates for a moment, but* **Fin** *encourages her to start.*

Maru   Once there was a girl, who planted a garden, and it was beautiful. One day she grew a tree, a massive lush tree, but then there was a famine . . .

Fin *nods to encourage* **Maru** *to continue.*

Maru   Even though there was a famine her mum always managed to find some water to give to the tree, and the tree always provided them with fruit. But when her mum died, people started to just help themselves to the fruit to make money from it without watering it. Without giving anything back. Until everything got so dry a crack appeared . . . and . . .

Fin   And?

Maru *shrugs as if to say 'I don't know'.*

Fin   And then one day . . .

Maru   The tree . . .

Fin   Yes, the tree . . . it . . .

Maru   . . . it . . . spoke.

Fin   It spoke and it said to the people of the village . . .

Maru   . . . to change their ways! It warned them and they listened. The people made peace with the tree?

Suddenly there is the sound of rupturing, a human hand appears from out of the crack, covered in dust and mud. Slowly a figure emerges, hauling itself up onto the other side of the **Crack** *to* **Fin** *and* **Maru**. *The figure is a young person about the same age as* **Fin** *and* **Maru**. *This is* **Asha** – *we recognise her as the young singer from the Prologue. She coughs, clearing her lungs, and wipes the grit from her eyes. She recoils in fear at the sight of* **Maru** *and* **Fin**, *who are equally shocked by* **Asha**'s *sudden appearance. Silence. They look at each other.*

Fin (*in disbelief*)   What is going on?

Asha *takes in her surroundings and spots the extent of the* **Crack***. She looks alarmed and becomes agitated.*

Asha (*shouting*)   Kwete, kwete zvakare! Izvi azvisi izvo! [*No, not again! This isn't right!*]

Fin   Shhh . . . be quiet! They'll hear you.

Asha (*almost angrily*)   The people made peace? You think that's how this ends?

Fin   Who are you?

Asha   I come from a village like the one in your story. I would pick fruit every day with my family, there was enough for each of us. Great Mother looked after us well.

But one day, men from far away places came. They offered our leaders money to grow tobacco on our land. So we cleared the fruit trees to make way for fields of leaves that no one could eat. When it came to harvest, the company would not pay what the tobacco was worth. We complained, over and over again, but our cries were ignored.

Then, the weather changed, a drought hit us and our remaining crops failed to produce. The earth was broken, groaning for help, until one day, it split! A crack appeared, just like this one. (*Pointing.*) It got so large that it started to consume everything. Homes. People. I was swallowed up by the splintered ground. But it seems the earth took pity on me . . . at least I am alive.

Maru   I'm so sorry. I don't know what to say.

Brunt   Come out, Maru! We can fix this.

Asha   Who's that?!

Fin   One of our brilliant leaders!

Asha   Then make them see how this might end.

Maru   We . . . we should tell them your story.

Asha   My story? My own people wouldn't listen to me, so why would anyone here take notice of what I've got to say?

Fin   Maru, I'm scared.

Maru   So am I.

Crowd (*off*)   I can hear them – they must be nearby!

Parent Two (*off*)   Maru!

Asha, **Maru** *and* **Fin** *are startled and afraid. The voices are coming from* **Asha***'s side of the* **Crack***.* **Asha** *looks around and spots a nearby plank. She places it over the* **Crack***.* **Asha** *crosses over the* **Crack** *to join* **Maru** *and* **Fin***, pulling the plank up behind her. She is just in time.*

Crowd (*off*)   Let's get them! They're over there, yes! Quickly! Come on!

Brunt *approaches with his* **Aide**, *and* **Maru**'s *family. A* **Crowd** *gathers quickly and there is tension with boos and shouts of confusion as they discover* **Fin** *and* **Maru** *on the other side of the* **Crack**.

Crowd   There they are!

Brunt   Good citizens, I come to you tonight not as your leader, but as a neighbour, a parent and your friend. Let me begin by expressing my deepest condolences to those who have suffered as a result of these cracks. Family members have been lost. Homes have been destroyed. Businesses have disappeared.

The **Crowd** *calms down and begins to listen.* **Brunt**'s **Aide** *is sipping from a branded fast-food paper cup.*

Brunt   There will be a time for grieving. But right now, we need to take back our city from those who would seek to harm us.

Eco-terrorists are capturing the minds of our young, exploiting their naivety. Do not be fooled by their 'facts' and statistics – these people do not share our values! They are weeds, intent on choking the life out of our future. And where do weeds reside? In the cracks!

Rest assured that these weeds will be identified, rooted out and destroyed. We say: 'Let our children be children, and leave the politics to us!'

The **Crowd** *claps and starts to cheer.*

Brunt   Elect me as your Mayor, and I will fill in the cracks! We will use concrete, concrete mixed and poured by local labour! Yes, we will create opportunity where they planned ruination! We will build over these cracks – shopping malls to rival the best, housing for our workers, support for local families –

Asha   What about *our* families?! What about *my* family?!

They **All** *turn and look at* **Asha**. **Asha** *steps forward.*

Asha   I've lost my father, my grandmother, my brother! Others have lost their homes, their livelihoods. My life is not a fairy story in a book for children. You live your lives without any sense of what the choices you make might mean for people like me, living on the other side of the planet!

Brunt   People like you? Other side of the planet?

Crowd One *(smoking)*   If you don't like it, go back to where you came from!

Asha   I would love to go home. But my home no longer exists.

Brunt *(turning to* **Aide***)*   Who is this child?

Asha   My name is Asha. My family died just trying to survive.

The cigarettes you smoke, the clothes you wear, the food you eat, the coffee you drink. Where do you think they come from? You take and you take and you take and you buy and you take yet more again until we . . . until the earth that we all live on can't give any more.

Brunt   Young lady, I can assure you that my plans have got nothing whatsoever to do with wherever it is you come from!

Asha   The decisions you make impact on the future of us all.

Brunt   You can't see the future! Certainly not the future of our fine city!

Beat.

(*To* **Crowd**.) I always say, everyone is welcome here, but we will not have negative attitudes undermining British values!

The **Crowd** *claps and starts to cheer.*

Asha *stands her ground.*

Brunt   We will rebuild. We will welcome a new wave of multi-national partnerships, the likes of which has never been seen before! We'll improve transport by investing in car manufacturing – electric cars to support *our* environmental objectives, *our* local needs and *our* future prosperity!

Maru (*walking out onto the plank*)   You're not listening to what she's saying! It's not the earth that's dying, we are!

The **Crowd** *gasp.*

Parent Two   Maru, it's going to be alright!

Maru   No, it's not, Everything is *not* alright! There are cracks all over the world, in places like Asha's village and on every other continent.

Parent One (*under her breath*)   Maru! Get back over here!

Maru   No. We need to *do* something!

Parent One   You can hardly breathe without the help of an inhaler, what are you going to do?

Maru   That's exactly why we need to act.

Crowd Two   Haven't you been listening? He's already said – electric cars!

Parent Two   We've got to trust the people in charge, Maru. They know what they're doing.

Maru   No – the people in charge aren't doing enough. We need more than electric cars!

Crowd One   Alright, little Miss Perfect!

Fin   It's not about being perfect, it's about starting to change how we behave . . .

Maru   I think we are scared. Our city is fragmenting before our eyes.

Crowd Three   Only because of people like you! With your doom and your gloom!

Maru   Why aren't you listening? It's not people like me – it's all of us – we need to work together!

Brunt   Why can't you just shut up, go home, and let us clear up this mess, so we can get back to normal and get on with our lives?

Maru   That's just it – we close our eyes and carry on as 'normal', filling the cracks – in our homes, our families, our lives – with things. A new iPhone, the latest clothes, takeaways on a Friday night. And another crack appears, and we close our eyes and carry on, round and round and round, filling the cracks again and again and again! Until there's nothing left to fill the void . . .

Helicopters are circling overhead.

The **Journalist** *returns with their* **Camera Person**.

Parent One (*desperate*)   Maru. You're risking your future! Please!

Crowd Three   It's your generation that insists on having everything brand new!

Maru   Listen!

Aide   I've saved for these trainers – you saying I shouldn't have nice shoes?

Crowd Two   Yeah, we all work hard!

Maru   You're not listening!

Crowd Three   And we all pay our way.

Crowd Two   You saying we don't deserve a holiday? It's only once a year!

Maru   No. I'm not saying –

Crowd Four   Why shouldn't I have the latest iPhone?

Crowd Two   They wouldn't make them if we didn't need them!

Maru *wavers.*

Crowd Three   If I start recycling now, what difference is it gonna make?

Crowd One   No one else bothers and it all ends up in the rubbish tip anyway!

Asha *joins* **Maru** *on the plank.*

Asha (*singing*)
    If ever it may seem
    Like there may be no tomorrow,
    Plant one small seed
    It may grow to feed a village.

Aide   What's she singing for?

Brunt's **Aide** *drops their takeaway cup in the* **Crack**.

The earth groans, the plank shakes, **Maru** *and* **Asha** *teeter over the chasm.*

Everyone gasps.

Maru   Listen.

Crowd Two   We've heard what you've got to say.

Maru   No – don't listen to me. Listen to the earth.

Aide   Now she's really lost it.

Maru   Can't you hear it? It's sobbing so hard, it's flooding our towns and cities. It's shouting so loud that fires rage though our forests and woodlands. The earth is cracking up and melting down. Right before our eyes. It's desperate to be heard. But you can't hear it. Whatever it does, we just carry on the same, giving it not even the slightest sign that we're willing to change.

Maru *turns, defeated, and walks back to where* **Fin** *is standing.*

Luca *approaches the opposite end of the plank and very carefully starts to cross. The* **Crowd** *gasp and object.* **Maru** *turns to watch.*

Luca (*arriving at the other side and grabbing* **Maru**)   I am. I'm willing to change. I could try meat-free Mondays from now on?

Maru *and* **Luca** *hug.*

Parent Two (*calling from the other side of the* **Crack**, *with the* **Crowd** *continuing to object*)   It wouldn't hurt me to start walking to work.

Parent Two *starts to cross the plank, pauses to look back at the crowd, then continues.* **Maru** *is grateful.*

Parent Two   And maybe we could cook together on a Friday night.

Crowd Three (*rushing to the middle of the plank and then stopping to regain balance as the* **Crowd** *object most to one of their own abandoning the cause*)   Yeah, OK, I guess I could take the kids to Margate this year, for their summer holidays, instead of Marbella.

Asha   We all need to work together.

Parent One   What about it, Bobby? What if your factories made electric buses . . . get us all out of our individual bubbles?

Pause as **Brunt** *tries to appear composed and unflustered.*

Brunt   Well, obviously, I have a five-stage plan . . . (*Looking at* **Aide** *for support.*) No-one cares about the environment more than me . . .

The **Crowd** *turn on him, hostile and full of questions such as 'Why shouldn't I have a new phone?', 'You promised us jobs!', and 'What you gonna do, Bobby?'* **Brunt** *is overwhelmed and tries to pacify them.*

Maru *and* **Fin** *speak over the hum of the general hubbub.*

Fin   Is this how it ends?

Maru   No, this is how it starts.

Asha *draws a calabash from the folds of her cloth and starts to sing the libation to Mother Earth from the start of the play.*

Others are drawn to her – first **Maru** *and* **Fin**, *then* **Luca**, **Parent Two**, *then* **Crowd Three**, *one or two others – but they don't know how to join in.*

Asha *starts to feed them, the new community, the lines – as the rest of the* **Crowd** *are slowly silenced, whilst remaining resistant to joining in.*

Asha   Great Mother!
Great Mother! We thank you, Great Mother!
You, who with loving hands, sculpts the clay from your earthy womb
(*Singing as if to indicate the others should join, but they don't understand.*) Form us!
Who, from your verdant sanctuary, yield both root and fruit
(*Quietly and to those gathering.*) Feed us!

Maru/Fin (*tentatively*)   Feed us!

Asha   Who, in your ancient wisdom, sends both storm and flower
(*Quietly and to those gathering.*) Teach us!

Maru/Fin/Parent Two/Luca (*building confidence*)   Teach us!

Asha   Who, with graceful force, forges rocks and continents
(*Quietly and to those gathering.*) Shield us!

Maru/Fin/Parent Two/Luca/Crowd Three (*with full commitment*)   Shield us!

End of play.

Great Mother (Prologue)

Free form

Great Mo - ther!_ Gre - at Mo - ther!_ We thank you, Great Mo - ther!_

You,_ who with lo - ving hands,_ sculpts the clay_ from your ear - thy wo -

mb, Form u - us!

Who,_ from your ver - dant sanc - tua - ry, yield both root and frui -

t, Feed u - us!

Who,_ in your an - cient wi - is - dom, sends both sto - rm and

flower, Teach u - us!

Who, with grace - ful force,_ for - ges rocks and con - ti - ne -

ents, Shield u - us!

You are_ the mo - ther, we are_ the chil - dren, Hear our prayer!
N - di - ni mai va - cho, i - su ti - ri va - na, Hear our prayer!

To those who came be - fore__ Those who lit our__ wa - ay

Let us ho - nour__ your me - mo - ry__

Let us car - ry__ your stories

For we who__ are blessed to__ be here and__ now__ May we be

mind - ful of our le - ga - cy - y.

Con - si - der those who__ are yet to__ come__

And tend the gar - dens of to - mor - row.

For the chil - dren of our fu - tu - re We pray you have the

con - fi - dence_ To stand strong_ in the ga - le But

yet the__ hu - mi - li - ty__ to bend in__ the breeze.

If ever it may seem (Scene 3)

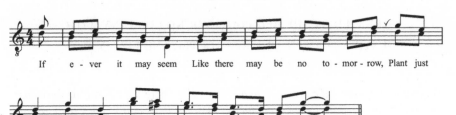

If   e - ver   it   may seem   Like there   may   be   no   to - mor - row, Plant just

one   small   seed,   It   may   grow   to feed   a   vil - lage.

Like There's No Tomorrow

CREATED BY THE BELGRADE YOUNG COMPANY WITH
JUSTINE THEMEN, CLAIRE PROCTER AND LIZ MYTTON

Summary of a recorded conversation between Like There's No Tomorrow *creators Justine Themen, Claire Procter and members of the Belgrade Young Company and director Sally Cookson*

The Belgrade Theatre's Young Company work with 200 young people each week. For this particular project, the Belgrade team wanted to make a full-length piece of work. *Like There's No Tomorrow* was made with a company of twelve young people living in and around Coventry, alongside co-directors Justine Themen and Claire Procter, and writer Liz Mytton. At the start of rehearsals, they didn't have a story in place; they just knew that they would be making a show about the environment. This meant that each of the young people involved felt a really strong sense of ownership of the play. At the time of making the show, the Friday school strikes were in full swing and it felt important to everyone involved that they made something that speaks to young people around the country.

The company wanted the play to reflect the power of stories in connecting us to each other and the world around us. Through stories we are able to make sense of our reality and begin to imagine it differently.

Company members brought their own stories into the rehearsal room. They also researched culturally-specific folk stories that explore humans' relationship with the Earth, and the spirituality and rituals that have largely been forgotten in the West. The exploration of these stories was a formative part of the process, helping to shape both the Prologue and Asha's journey.

Throughout the making of the show, the company found themselves becoming increasingly aware of small acts they could do themselves to help the environment – going round their homes switching off the lights, not using tea bags – but also thinking more and more about the structural problems in Western society and how these take us away from our natural environment. The biggest responsibility we have as citizens is to hold those in power accountable.

Notes on rehearsal and staging, drawn from a workshop with the creators held on Zoom in November 2020.

Sally Cookson, facilitating director, highlighted the fact that *Like There's No Tomorrow* had been created as a piece of devised work with the company. As a result, collaboration is at the heart of the play and it needs to be part of the creative process of staging it. Directing can be a lonely role, and it's important to acknowledge that for yourselves as directors, but also for your casts. It's important that your actors know that you don't have all the answers, and that they feel empowered themselves – this is true whether you're working with young people or professionals.

Preparing to direct the play

Sally offered up some exercises that she would use in getting ready to direct this, or any play.

First of all, she always allows herself one time reading the script just for pleasure. She thinks about her gut response, and notes what's pinged out to her about the story and themes. She reads it a couple more times, then starts to compile a list of information that's going to 'help me get under the skin of the piece'. This doesn't have to be an academic exercise (although it absolutely can be), but is as much about emotional responses: Sally makes music playlists, lists of films, artwork and other plays, as well as research (see suggested references at the end of these notes as a starting point).

Sally then asks herself: *why do I want to direct this play?*

Sally led the following exercise.

Exercise

- Spend five minutes asking yourself: why do I want to direct this play?
- Come up with a succinct, simple, understandable sentence – don't try to be clever.
- It only needs to make sense to *you* – there's no right or wrong answer.

A Zoom warm-up

- Stand with your feet in contact with the floor, transfer weight from one foot to another.
- Think about opening the top part of your bodies, housing the diaphragm.
- Move into a gentle jog.
- Imagine this is your one moment of running free, experiencing freedom.
- Open up voices, make some noise and feel that liberation for ten seconds.
- Back to slow transfer of weight from one foot to another.
- Slow down, come to sitting, reconnect with the screen.
- Connect with everyone else – pick up on the change in physicality as you all look back at the screen.

- Come back to a normal rhythm of breathing; think about the change to your body and brain.
- Go back to your sentence and *learn* it so you can say it confidently, passionately, clearly to anyone who ever asks you, 'Why do you want to direct this play?' This is about learning to *own* that sentence. There's no right or wrong.

Sally invited each of the directors to stand and share their sentence beginning, 'I want to direct this play because . . .' Some answers were:

- '. . . it speaks so clearly about the world today.'
- '. . . I want my students to have a sense of the wider world, and I like the rhythm and movement and storytelling of the piece.'
- '. . . I want to share the hope'
- '. . . it gives a platform and opportunity to young people who have a lot to say about our world.'
- '. . . it asks questions, gives young people the opportunity to navigate questions we're facing in our community.'

Through the exercise, Sally encouraged the directors to keep the energy throughout the sentence.

The collective voice

Sally highlighted the fact that, as well as you as a director knowing what's driving you to direct the play, it's also vital that the young people feel that they have a voice. As an ensemble piece, the company is a collective, a group of people with shared responsibility for a story. But there's a tension between the 'beast of the collective' (as Canadian choreographer Crystal Pite describes it) versus the individual performer. The individuals are as important as the collective voice, so how do you keep this in balance?

Events and challenges

Sally noted that in the group's 'Why I want to direct the play' sentences, many directors had said they were looking forward to exploring some of the most frightening things, the theatrical challenges of the play. Before going into rehearsals, Sally would always make a list of the big theatrical challenges – the problems that need to be solved to make the play the best it can be.

The directors talked about what they thought were the biggest challenges:

The crack

Sally noted that the crack is a lovely, knotty, seemingly impossible thing to put on stage, and the seemingly impossible is a spur to the imagination. The directors talked about what the crack could mean:

- It's like a scar on society.
- All those things that have been ignored, the things that have been left unsaid but should have been said.
- Cracks in the earth happen because something massive is happening under the surface.
- A disconnect in society and relationships, and the way the earth is used.
- If it could talk, it'd say: 'I'm hurting', 'Stop', 'I'm frightened'.

The group talked about how to represent the crack on stage:

- Using material?
- Make it physical, use the whole ensemble?
- Sally noted that the last character on the cast list is the 'Crack' – this is a clue for the director!

Sally suggested that she wouldn't make a decision straight away, but she'd hold onto those initial thoughts, and start talking about it with other creatives and the company. It's helpful to start engaging with these big challenges early on – spend sessions right at the beginning exploring them. It's definitely worth trying a lot of different approaches, and asking the company to come up with solutions. This helps develop a shared understanding of how you might realise that challenge. Then the rest of the piece can fit round that theatrical language.

Justine, Claire and the Belgrade company added that the whole show was made through asking the questions they didn't know the answers to in the rehearsal room.

Transitions between scenes

Sally suggested that it's important to see the links between scenes as scenes in themselves – they give you information about the story. They also add a real opportunity to create an ensemble and explore the style of the piece with the company. She encouraged the directors to be bold and play in the space. Sally shared a video from Crystal Pite's production of *The Seasons' Canon* – 'Autumn'. The directors noted that although the pace of the movement was quite slow, the dancers' intentions felt very alive and dynamic. Even simply walking across the space can be really powerful, if performers are connected physically and mentally. Simple exercises can unlock seismic challenges as theatre-makers.

Maru's cough

Sally noted that the cough has got to build and develop throughout the show, and that's really difficult for the actor playing Maru as it'll take a toll on their voice. Further, the cough has a theatrical significance; it isn't just a filmic moment, but a reflection of the sickness of the world Maru lives in. A naturalistic cough, by itself, is uninteresting. Can the ensemble help you realise it?

The Prologue

Sally invited the team from the Belgrade to talk about the making of the Prologue. They noted that it's important the Prologue should be related to the company. Anyone looking at the play should talk about it in relation to the company you're working with; Zimbabwe was the setting for the Belgrade production because one cast member had family there. What's crucial is that, compared with people in Coventry, the Zimbabwe setting offers more recent experience of a community living in harmony with each other, and harmony with the earth. There are some words in the Prologue in a Zimbabwean language, but these could be put in any language and/or translated back into English. The calabash is a symbol of giving things back that we have taken; the ritual could shift. Although there is reference to a 'Mother', the company are keen to have a ritual that isn't overly gendered.

It's important for the play that the earth is a living, breathing entity, and every culture relates to nature in a different way. In making the Belgrade production, everyone got excited about researching their own roots, and thinking about the relationship their own culture had with the earth – regardless of their own individual experience.

Uniting

In planning your production, Sally suggested it's always helpful to divide the play up into smaller units, in order to make it easier to think about your work. She looked at the opening sequence: the Prologue into Scene One. Scene One is quite a long scene with several locations and several links. Once you get to the City there are several sections:

- The link from Zimbabwe into the City
- The link from the City into the School
- The School into the City, with the Campaigners
- The Campaigners into the Park.

The Prologue is a clear scene by itself, and then the City is Scene One. Sally noted that it's important to be clear about *which* city you're setting the play in – to be as specific with yourself as possible. Sally would give titles to each unit to help her and the company focus on them. She'd use the following titles for the opening:

- Metropolis One
- School (Maru's cough is introduced and the crack appears for the first time)
- Metropolis Two (Campaigners)
- Metropolis Three (Link)
- The Park
- Metropolis Four (Link from the Park into Maru's home)

In order for the transitions to take place fluidly, it's useful to stay simple. Making environments with too much detail is going to make it hard to move fluidly from one scene to another. If you don't have someone to help you with the stage design, you can ask the students to help.

The rehearsal room

Sally always starts rehearsals with a warm-up for about half an hour. With young companies you may not have so much time, but even ten minutes allows people to leave the day they've had at the door and engage their creativity and sense of play. Sally's warm-ups always involve a combination of movement, an ensemble exercise and collective singing.

Once you've warmed up, it's helpful to spend a bit of time inviting the company's individual responses to the play. Sit in a circle and put the play in the middle, then go round the circle. Invite everyone to talk about what the play's about and ask what it makes them think about in their own lives. Pull ideas from everyone in the room about their own experiences.

After that, ask everyone to start researching. Give everyone something to do – this both helps broaden the range of research and also ensures everyone is part of the process.

I come from

A bit later in rehearsals, when there's trust between the group, Sally always runs this exercise. She was introduced to it by movement director Dan Canham.

- Put music on (Sally suggests this music is as neutral as possible).
- Take paper and a pen.
- For ten minutes, allow your thoughts to not be censored. Don't really think about what you're writing.
- Write a series of sentences that start with 'I come from'.
- The responses don't have to be literal – they can be words, thoughts, ideas.
- Make something that you're happy to share.

After ten minutes, the directors shared back their answers. They felt like there was a whole play in it already! They felt their experience of writing got easier as they went through, and that it was freeing to have a simple prompt and not be led through it in too much detail. One director mentioned they'd done a similar exercise using the prompt 'I want to live in a world where . . .' with their young people, which had been very powerful. Sally noted that this is something you can do as the individual performers, but also in character.

Visualising the character

Sally shared another exercise about getting into a character, thinking about who they are and how they're different to you. Each director was asked to choose a character from the cast list for this exercise; they were invited to turn off their screens and close their eyes.

- Imagine this character: see them in front of you.
- Give them a name if they don't have one already.

- Give them a specific age.
- Look at what they're wearing: how do they dress?
- If they have a job, what do they do?
- Where do they live? What sort of house do they come from?
- How does their day start? What's the first thing they do when they get out of bed?
- How do they get out of the front door? Do they have breakfast? Eat healthily? Make a packed lunch? Do they have jobs to do before they leave the house?
- How do they travel? Drive, walk, cycle?
- How do they connect to other people in their lives? Who's important to them? Who do they feel safe with, close to?
- Do they enjoy their time, where they have to spend time?
- Take the character on a journey, really observe how they go about their day to day lives
- Allow yourself to take on some of the physicality of this character. If they're younger or older than you, how does it affect the way they move, breathe, their rhythm?
- What does this character want out of their life? What would they tell you?
- What do they want for themselves, what do they want to achieve? Put it into a sentence that starts with 'I want'. Make it as simple and efficient as possible.
- Once you've decided it, keep repeating it to yourself in your head. It's going to be something that fuels and drives you.
- Introduce yourself to the group, as this character, and say what you want.

Some of the directors' introductions were:

- 'My name's Bobby, I want to remind each of you that I am for you, I'm here for the people.'
- 'I'm Phil, I'm a cameraman, I just want an easy life.'
- 'I'm Charlie the Chancer, and I just want to make a bob or two.'
- 'I'm Pamela, I work in HR and I'm a mum, and I just want to go on a spa break and not have a sick child anymore. I want to be me again, that's what I would like.'

Sally noted that this exercise is really useful especially when actors have quite small parts. It's a moment to really engage with the character, and also a great way of using the personality of the actor.

Sustainability

Sally shared an organisation called Staging Change, set up by a young sound designer. Given the subject matter of the show, it feels really important that the design and everything you use in it is, and feels, sustainable. Staging Change's website is: https://www.stagingchange.com/

Challenges

Sally reiterated that directing can be quite isolating when you're working on a piece, and that sometimes it's helpful to imagine bigger challenges to overcome! She divided the directors into breakout rooms, each with a title of something that may appear to be impossible to put onstage. As a group, they were invited to brainstorm ideas of how you might stage something really challenging. The groups were:

- A woman vomiting cockroaches (from *The Witches of Eastwick*)
- A volcano erupting
- A gigantic baby tearing the heads off a couple of people (from *Gargantua* by Carl Grose)
- Someone eating a rat (*The Monstrum* by Kellie Smith)
- Love dying

In the discussion afterwards, some solutions included: releasing smells into the audience, using sound with the lights right down, having the whole company wilt to the floor onstage, using slow motion, representing a tiny part of the horrific image, e.g. a rat tail coming out of someone's mouth, or going in the opposite direction and having the whole company embody rats all over the stage in a game of tag.

The other challenges directors discussed was how to respond to Covid-19 in rehearsals. Many young people might not have internet access at home so online learning engagement could be quite low. Solutions offered included:

- Send out creative challenges using letters and postcards (New Perspectives and Chickenshed both did this during lockdown).
- Run lines with young people over the telephone: call a parent's phone and ask them to pass it to the young person.
- Enlist your students' families to rehearse and run lines with them, then share it with the company as a radio play or invite them to send in video.

Questions and answers with the Belgrade team

Q: It's clearly an ensemble play, but there are clear stage directions for entrances and exits. In the Belgrade production, were the cast onstage all the time?

A: A combination. Mostly people went offstage after a scene, but there were some scenes where people stayed on ready to move into the next section. Trust your instinct.

Q: Is it important for the cast to make the prologue relevant to their own heritages? I have an all-Caucasian cast. Sticking to the script, the Zimbabwe setting offers possibilities for exploration of different cultures.

A: The essence is more important than the culture. In the Belgrade company, we were Black, white, South Asian. You don't have to set it in Zimbabwe, and you can adapt the language. The Iceland glacier funeral was also a useful reference for us, and everyone in that was white. Focus on the essence of the ritual.

Q: So, we can translate it into, for example, Scots if our kids connect to it?

A: Yes. But look at the opening and then Asha's speech. They need to be set from the same community, so consider both what's the ritual and what's the environmental impact. In our version we talk about fruit and tobacco, but it could be mining or fishing. We were talking about the West and the global South, but there are also issues right here in the West. Our text came out of personal discussions and researching into our own cultures was really important. Folklore is a really interesting project for cast members, including the folklore of the British Isles.

Comments from the Young Company members from the Belgrade:

- The topic is so pervasive, it was eye-opening to see the facts and experience them.
- Making the show felt really visceral; for example, a short thirty-second improvisation of ways in which people waste things led to a lot of reflection.
- It was a chance to recognise the power of storytelling, incorporating your own story into someone else's narrative.
- It made it really real to have those sessions around everyday scenarios. Climate change is such a huge thing, but it was so interesting to see how in our everyday lives we contribute to climate change, and how we can make a difference also.
- It's had a lasting effect on our lives and hopefully will have the same on the audience.

Sally encouraged everyone to be bold, to take risks and to encourage the young people to go as far as they can go. Justine reflected on the anxieties around Covid-19 and noted that the premiere performance in Coventry took place in the week that theatres closed in March 2020. This really shows that, if you've got challenges in putting the play on because of the context you're working in, that's a sign of the play speaking to the times we're in now.

Suggested references

Film

2040 (2019) dir. Damon Gameau
Documentary looking at the effects of climate change over the next twenty years.

An Inconvenient Truth (2006) by Al Gore
Concert/documentary film written by former US Vice President Al Gore, which prompts questions about climate crisis and global warming.

Koyaanisqatsi: Life Out of Balance (1982) dir. Godfrey Reggio
Experimental film exploring the imbalance between humans and the natural world, set to an original score by Philip Glass.

Writing

The death of a glacier:

https://www.bbc.co.uk/news/world-europe-49345912

https://www.stylist.co.uk/life/iceland-glacier-funeral-climate-change-global-warming-sea-ice-melt/288162

(News stories reporting on a funeral service held in Iceland to commemorate the loss of Okjokull, a 700-year-old glacier)

Field Notes from a Catastrophe: A Frontline Report on Climate Change by Elizabeth Kolbert (great introduction to the climate crisis and the impacts of global warming around the world)

How Bad Are Bananas? The Carbon Footprint of Everything by Mike Berners-Lee

Drawdown – The Most Comprehensive Plan Ever Proposed to Reverse Global Warming, edited by Paul Hawkin (bite-size summaries of policies, ideas and scientific developments that can help us to reverse global warming)

The Great Derangement: Climate Change and the Unthinkable by Amitav Ghosh (great on the interplay between patriarchy, capitalism, imperialism and the climate crisis)

What happens to our plastic?

https://www.independent.co.uk/environment/uk-plastic-pollution-oceans-recycling-export-waste-malaysia-vietnam-thailand-a8400761.html

https://www.theguardian.com/environment/2019/may/28/treated-like-trash-south-east-asia-vows-to-return-mountains-of-rubbish-from-west

(News stories on the impact of exporting some of the UK's recycling to South East Asia)

https://www.youtube.com/watch?v=GW7uORb9H8c&ab_channel=aerosceno

(Crystal Pite, *The Seasons' Canon* – 'Autumn', as referenced in the workshop)

From a workshop led by Sally Cookson, with Justine Themen,
Claire Procter and members of the Belgrade Young Company
With notes by Tom Mansfield

Participating Companies

20Twenty Connections
Aberystwyth Arts Centre Youth Theatre
Acorn Young People's Theatre
Act2 Academy
After-School R.O.C.K.S!
Alcester Academy
Ardclough Youth Theatre
Ark Alexandra
Artemis College
Artemis Studios
artsdepot Youth Theatre
ARTY
Astor Youth Theatre
BDC Company
Bedford College
Belgrade Young Company
Berzerk Productions
BHASVIC Theatre Company
Bilborough Sixth Form College
Black Sheep Collective CIC
Blue Bee Productions
Blue Elephant Young People's Theatre
Bluecoat Wollaton Academy
Brackley Youth Theatre
Brampton Manor Academy
Brewery Youth Theatre
Brilliant Theatre Arts
British School Jakarta
Broadland High Ormiston Academy
Bury Grammar School
CAPA College
Cast
Cheltenham Youth Theatre
Chichester Festival Youth Theatre
Chiswick School
Churchill Theatre Young Company
City of Oxford College
Cockburn School
Company of Teens
Congress Youth Theatre
Corn Exchange Newbury
Crescent Arts Youth Theatre
CWC Company
Cramlington Youth Dramatic Society
Cygnet Youth Theatre
Delanté Détras Theatre Company
Derby Theatre

Diocesan Drama Company
Drama House Ireland
DramaHubSussex and Bohunt!
Dudley College Performing Arts
Edinburgh Youth Theatre
Esher Church of England High School
Everyman Youth Theatre, Cardiff
Falkirk Youth Theatre
Farnborough College of Technology
Felpham Community College
Fisher Youth Theatre Group
Fleet Street Studio
Flying High Young Company
Framingham Earl High School
Greenbank High School
Group 64 Theatre for Young People
Gulbenkian Youth Company
Hackney Shed Ltd
Harrow Youth Theatre
Hawick High School Drama
Headington School Oxford
Heles School
Hinchley Wood School
Huntingdon Youth Theatre
Ilkley Players Greenroom
Imaginarium Theatre
Inspire
Kildare Youth Theatre
King Edward VI Grammar School
Kingsway Park HIgh School
Kola Nuts
Laguna Playhouse Youth Theatre
Lambeth Academy
Lammas School
Launch – Theatre and Performance Training
    at Cornwall College
Lavington School
Lincoln Young Company
Lipson Co-operative Academy
Lister
Lost Theatre
LUMOS Theatre
Lymm High School
MAAD
Mayflower Musical Youth Theatre
Mayflower Youth Theatre
Merchant Taylors School

Mishmak Youth Theatre
Multiplicity Theatre Company
New Vic Youth Theatre
Newcastle and South Tyneside Youth Theatre
NMPAT Young Actors Company
Norlington School
North Hertfordshire College
Nottingham College Actors
Nottingham Playhouse
Oaklands
Oldham College
On Hold Theatre Company
On Point Theatre Company
Ormiston Rivers Academy
OX2 Collective
PACE Theatre Company
PACT Theatre Company
Page2stage Community Group
Passmores Academy
Patrician Youth Theatre
Peake Productions
Pen and Paper Theatre Co. CYF
Perfect Circle Youth Theatre
Phenix Youth Theatre
Pike and Musket, Great Torrington
   School
Port Glasgow High School Drama Club
Prime Theatre
Pump House CYT
Queen Mary's College
ReACTions
Reading Studio of Dramatic Art
Redbridge Drama Centre
Reepham High School
Ringwood School
Roding Valley High School
Royal & Derngate
Rugby School
Ruislip High School
Saracens High School
Shaftesbury Theatre Youth Group
Shakespearia
Shazam Theatre Company SCIO
Sheffield People's Theatre
Shetland Youth Theatre
Siege of Herons
Silhouette Youth Theatre
Smithills School
Solihull Sixth Form College
Spotlight Drama Youth Theatre

Springwest Academy
SRWA Theatre company
St Mary's Catholic College
St Philip Howard Catholic School
St Saviour's and St Olave's School
St Thomas More Catholic High School
Stagecoach Cambridge and Cambourne
Stagecoach Chorleywood and
   Rickmansworth
Stagecoach Performing Arts Buckingham –
   Further Stages
Stagedoor Learning
Starmakers Dance and Performing Arts
Stockton Riverside College
Stratford Youth Theatre
Sundial Theatre Company
Telford Priory School
The Archer Players
The Boaty Theatre Company
The Community School of Auchterarder
The Customs House
The Drama Studio
The Garage
The Hayworth Players
The Heathland School
The John Lyon School
The Liverpool Empire Youth Theatre
The Repertory Theatre Project
The Sixth Form Bolton
The Swanage School
Theatre Royal Youth
Trinity College School
Trinity Youth Theatre
Union Youth Theatre
UROCK Theatre Company
Valley Park School
Vandyke Upper School
View From Here, Sawston Village
   College
Walthamstow School for Girls
West Lakes Academy
West Yorkshire Drama Academy
Westfield Arts College
Weymouth Drama Club Curtain Raisers
White City Youth Theatre
Wildcats
Windsor College
Winstanley College
Wisbech Grammar School
Woodrush High School

Worlds End Productions London
Worthing College
Wren Academy Sixth Form Drama Society
Yew Tree Youth Theatre
York Theatre Royal Youth Theatre

Young and Unique @ Callington Community
   College
Young Dramatic Arts
Youth Arts Centre, Isle of Man
Ysgol Aberconwy

Partner Theatres 2021

Aberystwyth Arts Centre
artsdepot
The Belgrade Theatre
Bristol Old Vic
Cast, Doncaster
Chapter Arts Centre
Chichester Festival Theatre
Derby Theatre
HOME Manchester
Hope Street Theatre
Lyric Hammersmith
Lyric Theatre, Belfast
Marlowe Theatre
MAST Mayflower Studios Southampton
Mulberry Schools Trust
North Wall, Oxford
Norwich Theatre
Nottingham Playhouse
Queens Theatre, Hornchurch
Riverbank Arts Centre
Royal & Derngate, Northampton
Sheffield Theatres
Soho Theatre
The Albany
The Garage, Norwich
Theatre Royal Plymouth
Traverse Theatre
Wiltshire Creative
York Theatre Royal

Performing Rights

*Application for permission to perform, etc. should be made before
rehearsals begin to the following representatives:*

For *Find a Partner!*
Independent Talent Group Ltd
40 Whitfield Street,
London
W1T 2RH

For *Like There's No Tomorrow*
Belgrade Theatre
Belgrade Square
Coventry
CV1 1GS

National Theatre Connections Team 2021

The National Theatre

National Theatre
Upper Ground
London SE1 9PX
Registered charity no: 224223

Director of the National Theatre
Rufus Norris
Executive Director
Lisa Burger